SCIENCE AND TECHNOLOGY EDUCATION
AND FUTURE HUMAN NEEDS

Volume 5

Education and Health

Science and Technology Education and Future Human Needs

General Editor: JOHN LEWIS
　　　Malvern College, United Kingdom

Related Pergamon Journal

INTERNATIONAL JOURNAL OF EDUCATIONAL
DEVELOPMENT

Editor: PHILIP TAYLOR

Throughout the world educational developments are taking place: developments in literacy, programmes in vocational education, in curriculum and teaching, in the economics of education and in educational administration.

It is the purpose of the *International Journal of Educational Development* to bring these developments to the attention of professionals in the field of education, with particular focus upon issues and problems of concern to those in the Third World. Concrete information, of interest to planners, practitioners and researchers, is presented in the form of articles, case studies and research reports.

Education and Health

Edited by

P. J. KELLY
University of Southampton, United Kingdom

and

J. L. LEWIS
Malvern College, United Kingdom

Project Leader

G. SCHAEFER
University of Hamburg, Federal Republic of Germany

Published for the

ICSU PRESS

by

PERGAMON PRESS

OXFORD · NEW YORK · BEIJING · FRANKFURT
SÃO PAULO · SYDNEY · TOKYO · TORONTO

U.K.	Pergamon Press, Headington Hill Hall, Oxford OX3 0BW, England
U.S.A.	Pergamon Press, Maxwell House, Fairview Park, Elmsford, New York 10523, U.S.A.
PEOPLE'S REPUBLIC OF CHINA	Pergamon Press, Room 4037, Qianmen Hotel, Beijing, People's Republic of China
FEDERAL REPUBLIC OF GERMANY	Pergamon Press, Hammerweg 6, D-6242 Kronberg, Federal Republic of Germany
BRAZIL	Pergamon Editora, Rua Eça de Queiros, 346, CEP 04011, Paraiso, São Paulo, Brazil
AUSTRALIA	Pergamon Press Australia, P.O. Box 544, Potts Point, N.S.W. 2011, Australia
JAPAN	Pergamon Press, 8th Floor, Matsuoka Central Building, 1-7-1 Nishishinjuku, Shinjuku-ku, Tokyo 160, Japan
CANADA	Pergamon Press Canada, Suite No. 271, 253 College Street, Toronto, Ontario, Canada M5T 1R5

Copyright © 1987 ICSU Press

First edition 1987

Library of Congress Cataloging-in-Publication Data

Education & health.
(Science and technology education and future human needs; vol. 5)
Papers from the Bangalore Conference on Science and Technology Education and Future Human Needs, organized by the Committee on the Teaching of Science of the International Council of Scientific Unions.
1. Health education—Congresses. 2. Health education—Case studies—Congresses.
I. Kelly, P.   II. Lewis, J. L. (John L.)   III. International Council of Scientific Unions. Committee on the Teaching of Science.   IV. Bangalore Conference on Science and Technology Education and Future Human Needs (1985)   V. Title: Education and health.   VI. Series.
RA440.A15E38   1987   613'.07'1   86-25525

British Library Cataloguing in Publication Data

Education & health.—(Science and technology education and future human needs; v 5).
1. Health education
I. Kelly, P.   II. Lewis, J. L.   III. Series
613'.07   RA440

ISBN 0-08-033946-8 Hardcover
ISBN 0-08-033947-6 Flexicover

Printed in Great Britain by A. Wheaton & Co. Ltd., Exeter

Foreword

The Bangalore Conference on "Science and Technology Education and Future Human Needs" was the result of extensive work over several years by the Committee on the Teaching of Science of the International Council of Scientific Unions. The Committee received considerable support from Unesco and the United Nations University, as well as a number of generous funding agencies.

Educational conferences have often concentrated on particular disciplines. The starting point at this Conference was those topics already identified as the most significant for development, namely Health; Food and Agriculture; Energy; Land, Water and Mineral Resources; Industry and Technology; the Environment; Information Transfer. Teams worked on each of these, examining the implications for education at all levels (primary, secondary, tertiary, adult and community education). The emphasis was on identifying techniques and resource material to give practical help to teachers in all countries in order to raise standards of education in those topics essential for development. As well as the topics listed above, there is also one concerned with the educational aspects of Ethics and Social Responsibility. The outcome of the Conference is this series of books, which can be used for follow-up meetings in each of the regions of the world and which can provide the basis for further development.

JOHN L. LEWIS
Secretary, ICSU-CTS

Contents

Part VII
Diseases of Global Importance

Part VIII
Other Papers

PART I

Introduction

Introduction

This book is the result of work done by the team working in Bangalore during August 1985 with representatives from all regions of the world.

Preliminary work had identified particular themes and the participants were divided into separate groups to work on each of these. For example, one group was particularly concerned with basic concepts, an examination of what precisely is meant by health, its contribution to the "quality of life" and how this should influence health education.

Another group of experienced educators dealt with environmental aspects of health, whilst another related old traditional styles of medicine to modern technologies and identified the importance of cultural influences. There was a group concerned with psychological aspects of health education and another with educational aspects of certain diseases of global importance.

As one of the planned outcomes was to produce new ideas, new approaches and new ways of teaching, a large number of case studies were identified and many of them will be found in this book so that everyone can benefit from the experiences of others. One active group was concerned with ethical aspects and the part such issues could play in health education. Such a gathering inevitably raises other matters of interest, teacher training, examinations, etc, and these contributions have also been included. In a subject as important as health education, it would not be right to concentrate exclusively on educational aspects to the exclusion of some straight science and there is included a paper on aspects of biotechnology which will no doubt become more significant in health education in the years ahead.

Reference to all the above will be found in this volume, which aims to reflect a holistic, dynamic and positive approach to the concept of health and to the teaching/learning processes in schools and elsewhere.

It must be stressed that the outcome of the workshops was very much a team effort and there was an input from many people which had a profound influence on many of the contributions even though they are not specifically referred to. The complete list of participants in Bangalore is listed in the first volume of this series.

At the Conference, there was a plenary address given by Shushila Nayar, who worked with Gandhi and whose influence on health education in India has been second to none. Her contribution was profound for it ensured that the discussions and the work of the group in general always had as a background to its deliberations the realities of what health education means in a rural part of a developing country. Her plenary address forms the rest of this introduction.

1

Health Education and Education for Health

S. NAYAR
Mahatma Gandhi Institute of Medical Sciences, Sevagram, India

I had the good fortune to learn health education and the delivery of health care to the community at the feet of Mahatma Gandhi, who may well be called the greatest scientist and saint of modern times. Science seeks truth and Gandhiji was a seeker of truth all his life. He had no use for abstract theories. He wanted science to solve the problems of the poor people in rural areas and in city slums.

We also learn that motivation of the community is most important to preserve and promote health. If people are sufficiently motivated, they will make full use of available health facilities and demand better facilities. But how do we motivate the community? Our experience has taught us that health is not, as a general rule, the first priority with poor villagers, though these are the people who need health care the most. They are too pre-occupied with problems of providing bread for the family. Poverty does not leave them time to think of anything else except how to make ends meet.

We may get angry with a mother for not taking her sick child to the hospital where free medical care is available. But the poor woman has to make a choice between going to the hospital and letting her other children starve, or going to work in order to feed her family, even though the sick child will get worse and may even die. She may often decide to leave the sick child to God's care. Can we blame her?

We may get angry with the head of the family who sells all the milk and eggs, not keeping any for his children. But he has to feed the whole family. He calculates how much money he can get from the milk and eggs and how much food grain he can buy with that money to satisfy the hunger of all members of his family. Can we blame him?

No, we have to think in terms of the removal of poverty. Health care, especially treatment of the sick, may serve as an entry point, but to motivate the community to preserve and promote their own health we have to help them to solve their economic problems.

5

There has to be a closer co-operation between health personnel and staff of other development departments. Health education and health awareness must permeate all development activities. It must also be borne in mind that economic development without health education will not solve the problems. We are all aware of the health problems of affluent societies, which result from over-eating, or wrong eating, or wrong living. Developing countries, on the other hand, have to think in terms of developing programmes that will enable them (a) to produce more, (b) to ensure that what is produced will meet the basic needs of life, and (c) to ensure social justice, so that there is fair distribution of the wealth produced. The purchasing capacity of the poor has to be improved.

Health and education departments are considered non-productive by our planners, and economies and cuts in expenditure are readily exercised with regard to them. In the health area, far more money is spent on hospitals to treat the sick than on health education or other preventive and promotive health measures. It is necessary to make the planners understand that, with good health and education, workers will be able to produce more in the fields and the factories. Health and education are an integral part of development.

Health habits, be they hygiene, proper nutrition, adequate exercise, rest or recreation can be taught by parents in the first instance, and then by school teachers. This implies careful training of teachers in health education.

What is health? Gandhiji in his "Key to Health", defined it as "Body Ease". The definition brings out the contrast to dis-ease. The World Health Organization has defined it as "A state of complete physical, mental and social well being and not merely an absence of diseases or infirmity". In our language, the word for health is "Swasthaya". It is made of two parts, *Swa* meaning self and *stha* meaning stability, so that health means "Stability within self".

The present-day consumer culture has to be replaced by what Gandhiji called the voluntary reduction of our wants. We must take to simple living and high thinking. Furthermore, we have to think not only of our generation, but also of generations to come. It has been said that God has created enough to meet man's need, but not enough for his greed.

Health is a basic need of life which enables full utilization of all other facilities to make life better, richer and more meaningful. It depends on a number of factors which fall in the area of action of departments other than health departments, as, for instance, proper nutrition, a healthy environment, adequate housing, purchasing capacity of the family and so on. It is therefore necessary that health education should permeate all strata of society: schools come first as the best medium, but education of physicians and others is also important.

Science education of our children makes them aware of mankind's responsibility to use natural resources wisely. The use of science and technology, tempered with wisdom, can prevent problems of pollution as well as of exploitation, and bring about prosperity for all. But peace and inner happiness are not dependent on prosperity alone. For achieving an era of peace and prosperity and inner joy, science must combine with certain basic values which can be summed up in one word "spirituality". This is the demand of our times.

PART II

The Concept of Health

Introduction

The first part of this section is concerned with the concept of health and its definition. After the first contribution which collects a variety of opinions, Professor Schaefer in the second identifies a holistic approach to health and at the same time he advocates strongly that a positive approach should be taken to it.

In the third paper, he identifies twelve principles of life as a basis for a positive concept of health.

Some interesting work was done by the Commission on Biological Education of the International Union of Biological Sciences using free association tests to find out students' attitudes and the next paper outlines the results of that work. This is followed by a description of similar work using a different technique with very young children in the UK.

The last contribution in this section, from Dr. Herbert Thier, reiterates again the proposal that there should be a swing from illness toward "wellness" when considering health.

2
What is Health?

The World Health Organization defines health as follows:

> "Health is the state of complete physical, mental and social well-being, and not merely the absence of disease and infirmity."

Some have regretted that this WHO definition of health is too static a formulation, others that it does not refer to two other factors which affect health, namely the natural environment and the transcendental property of the human mind.

M. R. Chakravarti from India describes his concept of health in the following way:

> "The fundamental determinants of health, apart from the genetic constitution, are nutrition, environment and lifestyle; the health of any rural Indian society is directly linked to its value system, cultural traditions, socio-economic set up and political organizations. Each of these has a profound influence on the health of an individual or community. Any health education programme cannot be limited to health care delivery, but should also be directed to bring about the cultural, economic, social and political transformation of the society as a whole, through the process of education."

Margaret Brumby from Australia writes as follows:

> "Our current research into students' perceptions of health, which involves extensive individual interviews where students explain *their* understanding of factors which they believe to be important to their own health, supports the emphasis on the health of the individual defined mainly in physical terms. Indeed when we asked them to explain what they thought would contribute to how long they would live, a completely new dimension of categories emerged – pollution, luck, accidents, war, heredity – all factors beyond an individual's control. What does this finding mean as to how students value the quality of their future lives?"

She also adds:

> "It is not very clear what WHO actually meant by the term 'social well-being'. Health education programmes seem to imply that 'social' means 'interpersonal'. Is not this a very narrow interpretation?"

Rex Meyer, also from Australia, writes:

> "The New South Wales educational system adopts a definition of health consistent with the WHO view. This concept of 'wellness' is reflected in the NSW definition that health is concerned with the total well-being of individuals and their ability to enjoy a healthy lifestyle."

The NSW curriculum unit called "Health Studies" defines health studies as:

> "that part of the curriculum which is concerned with the development of the total well-being of students and young people. It incorporates the curriculum areas of Dance, Health Education, Physical Education, Recreation and Sport and refers to aesthetic, emotional, intellectual, physical and social development."

Within the area of Health Studies, health education as such is defined more specifically as follows:

> "Health education provides learning experiences which influence understanding, attitudes and behaviour in regard to individual, home, school and community health."

The following diagram from the current NSW syllabus document summarizes this position:

Health education is dynamic in nature. Therefore, to be effective, it requires interaction between the individual, the home, the school and the community to increase the abilities of people to make informed decisions affecting their personal, family and community well-being, and this is reflected in the above.

In some countries, the prevention of disease is the major concern and when that is the case, it is reflected in the curriculum. K. C. Pang of the University of Hong Kong writes:

> "Health education is a method of conveying to the community the knowledge that is necessary for the prevention of disease, and the opportunity to lead a full normal life, physically, mentally and socially. This education should include:
> (a) a basic knowledge of the normal functioning of the body,
> (b) an understanding of the more common ailments,
> (c) the effects that certain habits have on the system."

Sushila Nayar in her plenary address, quoted in the introduction on page 5, refers to Mahatma Gandhi defining health by saying that "a healthy man has body-ease", thereby deliberately contrasting "body-ease" with "dis-ease". She also explains that the word "swasthaya" meaning health is made of two parts, "swa" meaning self and "stha" meaning stability – and "stability within self" is therefore perhaps the best translation of the word health.

3

The Total Human Health System

G. SCHAEFER

University of Hamburg, Federal Republic of Germany

The previous chapter has indicated some interpretations of the concept of health. In the planning for the Bangalore meeting and during the work in Bangalore it was agreed that Health had to be conceived as a *positive* concept, and not negatively as the mere absence of disease. This implies a holistic approach to health similar to that contained in the WHO definition of health as "the state of complete physical, mental and social well-being, and not merely the absence of disease and infirmity".

In contrast however to the WHO, there was a consensus that the areas relevant to health should be extended beyond the physical, mental and social boundaries, and should include the following two additions.

First, the natural environment: the non-social component of environment, like weather, radiation, water, food, diurnal and seasonal rhythms, etc, which have a marked influence on health.

Secondly, an extension of the mental factors, explicitly all the components of the conscious mind and also the large area of the subconscious. It is the totality of all psychological factors and their interrelationships for which the classical concept of "mind" is inadequate; the invisible area of life which transcends scientific enquiry, but which plays a vital role in the context of health, the transcendent, metaphysical, religious area.

The total human system responsible for health is regarded as having five major parts, namely:

physical,
mental,
social,
environmental,
transcendental.

Each part is conceived as an open sub-system. Each part interrelates with each other.

We conclude that health must be connected with some kind of stability of the whole system, which may be called "total health". Of course, in the development of the system there may be phases of partial neglect of one of the five parts, or phases of isolation of a sub-system, or of disturbed relationships between system parts. These phases of partial disease, however, can be counterbalanced by the total system, as long as this system is healthy, i.e. maintains its stability.

It has to be emphasized at this point that stability does not mean constancy or rigidity, i.e. a static condition, but rather an elastic one in which dynamic processes allow fluctuations between certain system-bound limits. This special kind of elasticity of a living system is normally called "biological equilibrium".

Partial disease can be overcome by a healthy total system if it exerts strong regulating forces. So the health of the whole seems dominant over the health of the parts. Accordingly, the final source of health of any living cell, organism, individual, community, population lies in the health of the whole.

Since health, like biological equilibrium, is not a static state, but a process, we have used a concept of dynamic health, which may be formulated as follows:

Health is the successful reaction to disturbance in a living system

This reaction type of definition seems very fruitful as it allows a patient to be defined, despite his ailments, as "still mainly healthy" as long as he or she is able to react appropriately to the disease. It also gives sense to the WHO's aim of "Health for All in the Year 2000", as indeed it is more realistic to achieve a positive, healthy way of reacting by the time indicated than a state of complete well-being (that is, without any disease), which will certainly never be achieved.

4

Twelve Principles of Life as a Basis for a Positive Concept of Health

G. SCHAEFER
University of Hamburg, Federal Republic of Germany

It has been found (see the work in Chapter 5) that the concept of health has negative connotations in West Germany and in some other industrialized countries. It is conceived as a negation of disease, whereas in other (mainly developing) countries the concept is of a more positive kind. Some countries regard health as a static phenomenon (the WHO defines it as the *state* of complete physical, mental and social well-being). Some look on health from a materialistic point of view (a physical phenomenon, achieved, maintained and repaired by material means such as medicine, food and medical equipment). Others think health to be mainly a spiritual phenomenon, a matter of attitude, of belief, of self-understanding.

With these diverging concepts, it is a challenge to find a basis for a positive, dynamic and holistic understanding of health. This basis can only be found when health is traced back to the very roots of life, so that in the end we can define health as the fulfilment of all basic principles of life. Or negatively expressed, if there is any serious and longlasting violence done against one of the basic principles sooner or later disease will result.

Piaget tried throughout his life to bridge the gaps between biology and psychology. He had a deep feeling for homologies between biological and intellectual structures and a belief that biological principles rule the living world at all levels of organization, including the social level and the world of the mind.

Normally in biology textbooks we find all or some of the following characteristics of living beings: growth, reproduction, metabolism, irritability, active movement, heredity and mutability. These are found in all organisms, but they are unsuitable for use in the psychological and sociological domains. We are in need of superordinate terms to describe basic processes underlying any kind of living phenomena, material or spiritual.

For this reason the basic principles of life described below are formulated on the abstract level of systems theory so that they may be applied and understood in different disciplines, and, in particular, form a link between science and humanities. This approach does not mean a fallback reducing humanities to biology ("biologism"), but the attempt to derive both areas of life sciences from the same formalized roots.

1. Entropy Reduction (Creation of Order)

Each living phenomenon is continuously counteracting the internal natural increase of entropy by means of energy conversion. Entropy is mainly exported on heat as a carrier, and energy of a higher quality has to be consumed (nutrition). This high-quality energy yields order to the living phenomenon which, in turn, is used to maintain and increase the living order.

This principle is probably not equivalent to the other; it is rather of a higher rank, because the basic structures of a living system and its capability to preserve these structures by continuous reduction of entropy – against the common trend of nature – are the most spectacular and unique properties of such systems. Most of the other principles of life seem to have a serving function only.

There is a certain "conservative trait" innate in all living beings with respect to order, the material basis of which is described by Mendelian genetics. Health education, however, has not only to develop a positive attitude of children towards maintenance and increase of order (or decrease of entropy, respectively), but also to the tolerance or even appreciation of partial disorder (Paul Valéry: "there are two great dangers threatening mankind: order and disorder"). Rigid order, without any flexibility, is as harmful to life as complete chaos; many examples from the history of the biosphere are proving this. It seems that life develops at its best if there is always a small and limited disorder, as a creative element, on a strong and reliable basis of order which gives security. This ambivalence of order/disorder, security/insecurity appears to be most favourable for life and to guarantee maximal reduction of entropy in the biosphere as a whole.

2. Reinforcement and Reproduction (by Positive Feedback)

Compartments or variables are able to increase or multiply (autocatalysis, exponential growth, etc) due to a mechanism of positive feedback (an effect reinforces its cause). However, positive feedback in reverse (negative feedback) may also lead to exponential decrease (decay, collapse, catastrophe), if a vital variable sinks down.

Although living systems may be stabilized as a whole and not grow or reproduce, there are always parts which do so. There is no cell without plasmatic growth, no organism without growth of certain tissues, no population of a minimum size without children, no economy without growth of capital and/or new technologies, ideas, strategies, etc, and no ecosystem without growing and reproducing populations, as long as these systems behave normally and are healthy. Growth and reproduction (the increase of biological substance) are necessary events in order to compensate for the continuous decay of living matter. In this respect, principle 2 is very closely related to principle 1. However, principle 1 is certainly superordinated to principle 2 as unlimited growth and unlimited reproduction very quickly lead to complete misbalance or disease and finally to death. So each reinforcement of biological substance and structure has to be controlled by regulation mechanisms (see principle 3), keeping the balance which we call "health".

3. Elasticity and Stability (by Negative Feedback)

Each living phenomenon has the capability of self-stabilization. This capability, sometimes called homeostasis, is a general effect of negative feedback (the effect diminishes its cause) functioning in contrast to positive feedback, equally in the opposite direction, to produce stability.

Without this ability to stabilize, a living system would be a victim of any kind of disturbance: it would either collapse or explode. Thus inhibiting processes in our life, although providing negative feedback, should always be acknowledged as making a contribution as they may be vital to the stability (the health) of the total system.

This aspect has consequences: normally people think predominantly in terms of growth provided it is their own and not the growth of others, and they do not expect to be hindered in this expansion. It requires an educational effort to make people realize that some amount of self-constraint and even sacrifice is necessary to keep the balance in the community and the ecosystem.

4. Adaptation

Each living phenomenon is able to adjust to its environment by different mechanisms. Either it adjusts external structures to its own structure by means of assimilation, or it adjusts its own structure to the environment by means of accommodation. In both cases the individuality of the phenomenon is maintained.

Adaptation is a variant of elasticity and necessary for health. Any rigidity or lack of flexibility, in body or mind, reduces the chance of finding the optimum of life, and so may lead to permanent stress and eventually disease. Appreciation of this is not self-evident, especially as adaptation may often require self-denial and the overcoming of traditional habits. So health education has to aim at preparing a readiness for adaptation. However, as for all other principles, there is a limit when a living phenomenon is threatened. Health needs adaptation, but it is not achieved by adaptation alone.

5. Individuality (Uniqueness)

Each living phenomenon is delineated from its surroundings by a semi-permeable surface (a skin). Furthermore, no living phenomenon is identical to any other; each of them is unique in the way that its composition of elements, its structure and its internal and external relationships are not completely reproducible.

Denying individuality of human beings by equalizing them in a mass society makes people sick after a while. Everybody wants to have their own personality, to have a demarcation from others, giving a minimum amount of security for their individual needs. So, supporting individuality means contributing to health.

6. Compartmentalization

Each living phenomenon has internal borders. However, the borders are not closed, but principally open to matter, energy or information. Living phenomena are characterized by open systems and sub-systems.

Isolation – whether of cells, organs, individuals, ecological systems, concepts, ideologies, emotions, the conscious from the subconscious, the individual from its environment – generally leads after a while to disease. So, the exchange of matter, energy, information between compartments means contributing to health. (This does not exclude, of course, the partial or temporary closing of a system if its entropy is increasing too much and principle 1 is violated.)

7. High Complexity and Interdependence

All parts within a living phenomenon are related to and dependent on each other. The number of mutual relationships is much greater than the number of parts.

If some kind of practised reductionism leads to homogenization of a living system and a diminished complexity, there is always a danger of isolation of parts (see 6) or suppression of individuality (see 1). Hence reduced complexity very easily leads to disintegration of the system and thus to disease or even death. Supporting high complexity in a living system means contributing to the health of the system.

8. Hierarchy (Priorities)

The different compartments and relationships within a living phenomenon are not equivalent with respect to survival and development. There are those with high importance, the key parts and key relationships, which can less easily be missed or changed, and those with a lower importance, which can more easily be missed, replaced or changed. There exists a hierarchy.

However, we live in a time of increasing equalization of people in an industrialized world, despite all that is said about individuals. We experience today attempts to abolish hierarchical structures in societies and to remove any kind of authority. We find unexpected after-effects of monocultures (fields, forests), of mass populations (chicken farms), of vast numbers of substitutes in our markets. People begin to feel ill and they do not know why.

Hierarchy in living systems means that there are different priorities. There are organs in our body which need more attention than others (the brain for example with respect to oxygen supply); there are in society people who need more attention than others (regeneration time for children, for example). There is always a ranking system in any healthy living being, and violation against this or its complete abolition leads to serious damage and disease.

9. Semantics

Living phenomena have the capability of codifying structures or variables by means of signals. They use certain structures or variables as carriers of a meaning (information). The use of objects as carriers of information is a miraculous phenomenon of life. Their existence may not be essential at the moment, but their existence is vital for the survival of any organism, as they help to recognize dangers in time.

10. Information Storage

Living phenomena store information by codifying it in durable carrier systems. By this method they are able to make use of present information at later times and thus overcome the "time barrier" to some extent. This principle is strongly connected with 1, the order principle.

As information is somehow a spiritual (non-material) principle in our world which has very precisely to be distinguished from its carriers (matter, energy, or charge), information storage means storage of something which is beyond the material world.

Positive health education has to take this notion of "inheritance", "continuity", "non-material thinking" into consideration. It is the author's conviction, born from a long experience with biocybernetic courses, that such a notion is promoting something like a "health of the mind", as it is stressing the spiritual side of the world which is the essence of the mind itself. That this attribute has a strong impact on learning needs no explanation.

11. Active Movement

Each living phenomenon is able to move actively (by its own impulse and energy resources) either totally or in parts. Movement means translocation in space and time and normally serves principles 1, 2, 3, 4, 7, 8, 9 and 12.

How much active movement is necessary for health needs no explanation. Intuitively, all children regard movement as the most characteristic property of living beings and hence very often even do not recognize plants to be alive. However, when referring to people every child feels the great importance of this principle. It is well-known how many diseases arise from a lack of movement (irregularities of the spine, circulation diseases, social isolation, etc). So a strong encouragement to move should be a vital part of positive health education.

12. Internality

Living phenomena, as judged from a human perspective, seem all to have a dimension of subjectivity which transcends the operational possibilities of science. It is a kind of consciousness, awareness, internal view which we know from ourselves and which, to some extent, we must also attribute to other living beings, although we can never prove this. Because of the impossibility of proof, principle 12 is not a scientific part of biology.

People have two possible ways of observing themselves: the scientific method, leading to all the disciplines of human biology, and the method of introspection, leading to disciplines like philosophy, the arts, the humanities. The latter disciplines make statements about feelings, perceptions, deliberations, sensations. All these are not objects of science as they can only be experienced personally.

If we are going to collect principles of life which are relevant for all its manifestations, both the physical and the spiritual ones, we cannot constrain our endeavours to the perspectives of science alone, but have to include the introspective disciplines as well. It seems quite essential for human beings to be acknowledged as subjects with internality and not to be degraded to some kind of machines which just function and are unable to enjoy, to suffer, to love. With respect to health, it is obvious that people do not feel well for long if they regard themselves as machines or blackboxes. All medical evidence proves the necessity of a psychological view for the maintenance of health. This is the basis for the development of an individual "psychosomatic medicine", and positive health education certainly has to devote much effort to this psychological aspect, as it must also develop something related to the "spiritual aspect".

Twelve Questions Arising from the Twelve Principles

If we take the above principles of life as a starting point for positive health education, we should ask ourselves the following questions, giving an answer to each. A positive attitude developed in students will manifest itself in a positive form of health care, but also in corresponding ways of treating environmental and other affairs.

(1) Are you willing to support, maintain and create order in our world? Which order, and for whom?

(2) Are you willing to tolerate and even support growth even if not in your own immediate interest? What growth do you accept or even demand from others?

(3) Are you willing to preserve living structures and living beings in order to maintain stability in our world? Which disturbance of living systems do you resist and which do you allow to happen?

(4) Are you willing to adapt to changing situations, instead of insisting on previous habits?

(5) Are you willing to tolerate and even appreciate other people's individuality and do you have the courage to develop your own, maybe against social pressure?

(6) Are you willing to recognize and also to sustain the great complexity of your internal and external life? Are you prepared to live with uncertainties, ambivalences or conflicts that are involved with this complexity?

(7) Are you willing to conceive the living world as a world of open systems, with open and transitional borders? Do you accept the opening-up or abolition of previously set strict limits on behalf of a richer and more creative life?

(8) Are you willing to accept the existence of hierarchies in the natural world and in your social and personal life? Do you allow others to set their own priorities, even for you, or do you take the risk of setting your own priorities, even on others, and bear the consequences?

(9) Do you conceive your world as a world of signs which have a meaning

for you? Are you willing to spend time and effort upon the elucidation of this meaning, even if it is hard to recognize?

(10) Do you actively support storage of information, by learning, writing, tape-recording? Are you willing not only to use technical media for information storage, but also to train your own memory?

(11) Are you willing to move, in a world of hundreds of technical temptations against movement?

(12) Are you convinced that you are not a body, but that you have a body? Do you believe that in yourself there is a spiritual core of pure internality that cannot be objectivized and thus be made the object of science? Are you willing to accept the tremendous loneliness that proceeds from the knowledge of being absolutely alone with your own subjectivity?

5

The Concept of Health: Free Association Tests

This chapter is based on an empirical study initiated by the IUBS Commission on Biological Education and on contributions by E. BAYDOUN, D. HERNANDEZ, G. SCHAEFER, I. STYRZ and J. WILLE.

For effective teaching it is important to know what previous understanding students have of a subject. Do they already understand key ideas on which new knowledge can be built? Have they beliefs or misunderstandings which will hinder the development of appropriate knowledge and attitudes? If the answers to such questions are known, relevant teaching programmes can be devised. If not, confusion and frustration can easily result. This is particularly important in health education which is not just concerned with passing on knowledge about health, but with ensuring that knowledge is translated into healthy attitudes and behaviour. For this reason it was necessary to find out about the associative frameworks of concepts concerned with health and an empirical study has been made by the Commission for Biological Education of the International Union of Biological Sciences.

The research was carried out in a number of countries. The samples studied were relatively small and thus cannot be seen as necessarily typical of the countries concerned; however it is significant that different patterns of association are shown by the different samples.

The Methodology

Upon a key-word, in this case "Health", the students write down spontaneously what comes to their mind. They are asked not to think or reflect about the key-word. (The technique can be applied simultaneously to other concepts, such as equilibrium, growth, energy, order, environment, etc, but our concern here is merely with the concept "Health".)

It transpired that this method of testing is an unusual one as far as schools are concerned as teachers do not imagine it can produce serious results: they feel it must be devoid of any logic. However, as a great part of life is indeed illogical and unsystematic compared with organized school knowledge, the free association test reflects this part of life and thus the reactions of students which are likely in real-life situations.

From all the associations given, those selected were the "emotionally loaded" ones, either positively or negatively. The positive ones were those centring around health (exercise, good food, smiling faces, happiness, sports, etc); the negative ones around disease (sickness, hospital, pain, doctor, etc). The total of positive and negative associations given below relate to this total. (The number of neutral associations which are neither positive nor negative (shape, body, condition, etc) amounted to only 2% of all the associations when the tests were done in Jordan, but to about 10% in West Berlin.)

The Results

Charts A and B show the reactions obtained to the key-word "Health" when the tests were conducted in West Germany: Chart A was based on 13-year-old children and Chart B with a wider range of people, aged 14–25. Charts C and D show the equivalent results in the Philippines. The shaded regions show the associations which were negative, the white regions the associations which were positive.

It is significant that in West Germany the dominating reactions centred around disease rather than health, whereas in the Philippines the reactions are the other way round.

The results for Barbados, Canada and Jordan are shown in Charts E, F and G and are in between the two extremes, although they incline more towards the health side than disease, as was the case in the Philippines. Perhaps a surprising result, Japan, although a highly industrialized country, showed a strongly positive concept of health as shown in Chart H.

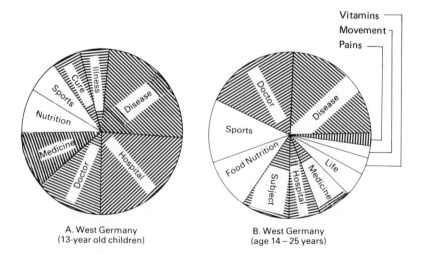

A. West Germany
(13-year old children)

B. West Germany
(age 14 – 25 years)

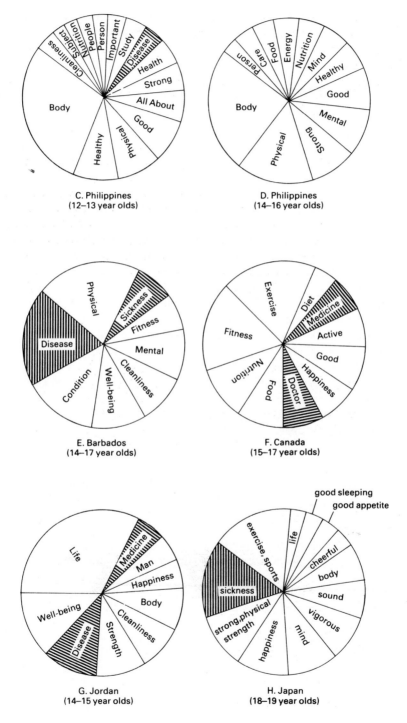

C. Philippines
(12–13 year olds)

D. Philippines
(14–16 year olds)

E. Barbados
(14–17 year olds)

F. Canada
(15–17 year olds)

G. Jordan
(14–15 year olds)

H. Japan
(18–19 year olds)

So the positive and negative connotation of Health is not merely an effect of standards of living and medical health care, but seems to result from other factors.

Association Chains

Further work was done using chains of associations in which students wrote down a sequence of associations. The results obtained in Jordan and West Berlin are contrasted below.

The white columns represent the positive associations, the black columns the negative ones. The total sample of West Berlin shows a slight predominance of positive association at first, but from the third place onwards a predominance of negative ones. By contrast, in the total sample from Jordan, there is a predominance of positive associations over the whole chain, although the percentage of negative associations increases over the chain. Comparing the two results, we find a much more positive picture of associations around health in Jordan than in West Germany. If we compare girls and boys in West Berlin, we observe a slight and constant predominance of positive associations in girls, but a clear predominance of negative associations in boys, increasing across the chain. The same comparison in Jordan shows that here also the girls associate more positively than boys, but the difference is much greater than in West Germany. In addition the positive associations decrease continuously within the chain in girls, whereas they form a minimum in the case of boys with the lowest value at the third place in the chain.

It is interesting that there is a marked difference between the sexes in both populations, regardless of nationality. Girls have a more positive attitude and are more steady within the association chain; boys have a more negative attitude than the girls, but their negative associations pass through a maximum at the third or fourth place in the chain.

Comparing age levels in West Berlin, we find a striking increase of positive associations with increasing age. Young students show a predominance of negative associations, older students of positive ones. The inversion seems to occur around the age of 15 – see chart Q. At all age levels, the graph of the negative associations is mainly a maximum curve, with that of the positive ones a minimum. A similar comparison in Jordan reveals a comparable trend: here also the percentage of positive associations increases with the age of the students.

Conclusions

There appear to be four conclusions to be drawn from this investigation. First, the concept of health, as measured by free-association tests, has much more positive connotations in Jordan than in West Berlin. This

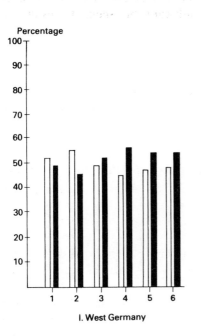

I. West Germany

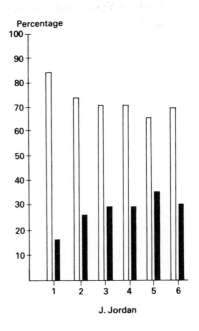

J. Jordan

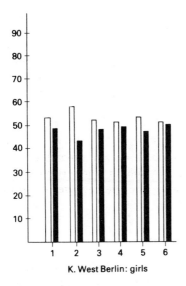

K. West Berlin: girls

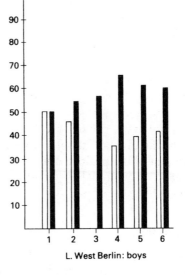

L. West Berlin: boys

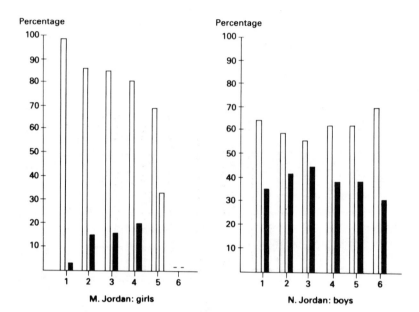

M. Jordan: girls

N. Jordan: boys

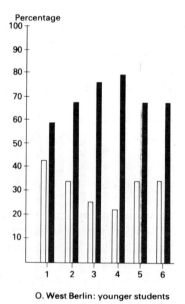

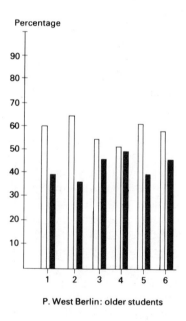

O. West Berlin: younger students

P. West Berlin: older students

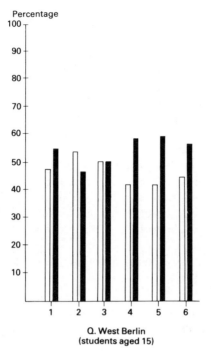

Q. West Berlin
(students aged 15)

difference can also be shown by comparing Amman with West Berlin, the two main cities, so it seems to be a national characteristic, not a matter of urban/rural populations. (This assumption is strongly supported in the Philippines where both rural and urban investigations showed much more positive associations than in West Germany.)

We may conclude, therefore, that developing countries have a much more positive attitude towards health because in these countries of scarce medical technology a positive attitude towards life and health is just a matter of survival. In the industrialized countries, on the other hand, nearly everybody can survive with the aid of doctors, hospitals and medicine, and without such a strong belief in one's own individual power. On the other hand, Japan is an exception as far as this hypothesis is concerned.

Secondly, the difference between the sexes is striking. Independent of country, there seems to be a tendency for females to have positive attitudes towards health, whereas there is a more negative attitude among males. Perhaps females think more positively about health because they are concerned with the internal forces of life and development for themselves and their family. Males, on the other hand, tend towards more external connotations of health, including the technical solutions for health problems.

Thirdly, an important result is the relatively high percentage of negative associations in young children, which decreases with increasing age in both Germany and Jordan. Normally one would expect the reverse: younger children are very often much more optimistic and positive in their views on life than older ones. According to interviews with pupils, parents and teachers in West Germany, the strong trend towards disease-centred associations (although the key-word was "health") in younger children may be due to the fact that they are more passive to the influences from their environment, for example, from parents' talk, advertisements, radio, TV, etc, and so they associate with health what they normally hear about loss of health and about disease, its therapy and prevention, a reaction which changes with age as a positive approach to health develops.

Fourthly, the general observation of maximum and minimum curves within the association chains indicates a process of compensation in the students' minds. It seems as if after a certain trend has taken place towards positive or negative associations a counter-trend develops.

6

Perceptions of Young Children Concerning Health

A. MOON, N. WETTON and D. T. WILLIAMS

Southampton University, UK

In order to find out what are the perceptions of young children (aged 4–8) concerning what makes and keeps them healthy, a simple research tool was devised and tested in 125 primary schools spread over the regions of England and Wales. The technique is based on that most frequently used classroom activity of early school, where children gather round the teacher and are introduced by her to some topic. She may pose a problem or ask them to recall or reflect on their own experience or activities. Then she will encourage them to make their own interpretation of their discussion in pictures and writing.

Writing at this stage is a new, difficult and complex activity and so the teacher at first will act as the writer, setting down for the children what they want to record or communicate. Later the activity of writing may be shared by children and teacher with the teacher as consultant, dictionary and occasionally secretary. Some children may then want to take on for themselves the responsibility of their own writing; others will be less confident and require continued teacher support.

The "draw and write" technique proved to be a success in finding out the values and beliefs of young children related to health. It brings the benefit of knowing "where the children are" as the starting point for teaching and learning. Too often health teachers (and teachers in other areas of the curriculum) start from the teachers' perceptions of children's needs.

For the purpose of the research, the activity was modified so that:
- talk was confined to the teacher, working from a set pattern of statements and instructions;
- the children were asked not to share in the discussion, but keep their ideas in their head;
- children's requests for help with writing would have to be spoken so that other children could not hear.

It was proposed that these modifications would best be carried out by

35

involving the children in a game of "secrets" asking them to make pictures inside their heads, keeping them secret until they turned them into drawings, to whisper their requests for help with their writing as part of the secrets game, and to hide their drawings from the other people's eyes.

The results were coded and analysed. Four typical drawings are illustrated. (Those children who had written for themselves present the research team with some problems of translation since they tend to spell phonetically: "ecsiyeing" for "exercising" in one of the examples shown.) Analysis indicated clear-cut trends in the children's response to the concept of "being healthy" and "keeping healthy". At the same time, it illuminated the strategies children used when faced with difficult concepts, particularly those of cause and effect. For some 20% of the children the answer was to shut out the difficult concept ("health") and to seek some everyday response in the task they had been set. So "Draw what you do to make you healthy and keep you healthy" was simplified by them into "Draw what you like". This they then did, with restored confidence, drawing robots, snowmen, my house, and me and my mum. Despite the fact that this provided insights into their strategies, these were coded as nil responses.

Setting aside the nil responses, there were 1,225 responses from 769 children (some drew more than one picture). Of these responses only 23 were concerned with prevention or cure of ill health (ranging from visiting the doctor, taking pills or tablets to having a plaster (the infant school panacea for many ills).

There were many responses for exercise, 417 in all; and 346 for food. Caring for teeth was next, followed by hygiene and sleep. (The hygiene category included all aspects of personal hygiene, washing, hair grooming, going to the lavatory, keeping the home clean.)

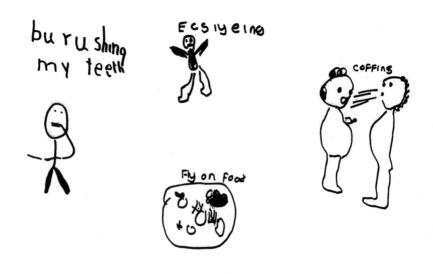

The study afforded insights into children's perceptions of being healthy in terms of their own activity. It showed clearly that they relate this to certain activities – exercising, eating and cleaning teeth. Why and how they make this relationship is seen to be a critical factor requiring further investigation. It was clear that dental health education had made a strong impact in certain schools.

7

From Illness to Wellness

H. THIER

Lawrence Hall of Science, University of California, USA

Historically one of the major foci of health education has been the nature of "illness" and how to treat it. Another traditional emphasis has been the prevention of disease, including recommendations for personal and community programmes, to accomplish this goal. In these aspects of health education substantial responsibility is delegated to the health professional with the individual acting in the role of the receiver of services. Health professionals are "service providers" and the individual has been the patient or client. Important and needed as these programmes are (especially in developing countries), they are only part of our present conception of a total health education programme.

Current trends in health education focus on "wellness" rather than "illness," and on the importance of decision-making by the individual in improving and maintaining the quality of his or her life; decision-making to help the individual, and the community as a whole, to live more healthfully. It includes purely personal decisions such as not smoking. It also includes acting as members of the community to encourage reduction of air pollution or possible exposure to toxic or hazardous substances. The emphasis is on the individual as a direct decision-maker regarding his or her personal health or wellness and as a concerned, involved citizen regarding those issues which affect the health or wellness of the community as a whole.

Treating illness and preventing disease are still vital issues, but are placed in a context of overall health education which has as its primary goal the encouraging of "wellness". In this conceptualization of health education, the professional health educator acts in the role of advisor and consultant to the individual and community regarding the decision-making process. In addition, they provide or make provision for instructional experiences so that the individual and/or community can accomplish their goals. An interesting, specific example of the possible scope of the role of the professional health educator is the evolving trend of industries to add health educators to the staff of their plants. These individuals, for example,

39

provide instruction regarding ways to foster healthful living at home, organize and carry out exercise and stress reduction programmes at work and in other ways provide opportunities for the individual to increase and maintain the quality of his or her life. Many companies claim all costs are paid for by improved morale, decreased absenteeism and decreased employee medical costs which lead to lower or controlled health insurance costs.

The approach is one of providing opportunities and expecting the individual to take advantage of them since it is not possible to meet all the goals of a "wellness" programme through a "service provider" orientation. Since there are so many more "well" than "ill" people, the "wellness" aspect of health/science education has primarily to be a "do it yourself job" with the individual taking major responsibility for maintaining his or her own well-being.

Educational Implications of a "Wellness" Emphasis

Encouraging wellness as a lifestyle requires a wide variety of educational inputs and opportunities throughout the individual's life. As new information or variants of old information become important in the community, the individual needs input in order to be able to make decisions as to what is best for personal well-being and the well-being of the community. This requires a developed professional infra-structure in the community responsible for research, public education, etc, regarding health and health-oriented issues. It is necessary to increase the population's interest in the willingness to learn about health and to increase the individual's capability to use evidence to make informed decisions if these ongoing community health programmes are to be successful. One important way to bring this about is to emphasize such topics and concerns in the pre-university formal and informal health/science education experiences of individuals.

Focusing on such goals in pre-university health/science education will lead to immediate informed decision-making such as the decision not to take up cigarette smoking. It will also lead to an adult population better able to sift, understand and make decisions about new issues that come up when they are adults regarding their own "wellness" and the "wellness" of the community.

Even if we knew the answers to all of today's health/science oriented issues (we don't) we cannot predict what new issues will come up in the future. Therefore, the emphasis of any instructional programme for the young in these areas has to be investigative, analytical and based on teaching the skills and processes of evidence-based decision-making at the same time as one tries to accomplish specific goals such as smoking prevention. Programmes developed and/or currently under development at the Lawrence Hall of Science (see page 161) are examples of the kind of subject matter and approaches necessary to accomplish the short- and long-term goals described above.

The goal is to develop intelligent "consumers" of health education. These individuals, when faced with decision-making, should value evidence over emotional appeals to help them reach decisions. For example, decisions regarding one's own health and lifestyle should be based on evidence after taking into consideration the short- and long-term risks and benefits of different decisions. This contrasts with the individual who is "guided" only by advertising. The instructional goal is to provide information and experience in ways that are of interest to individuals. This helps them see the value of evidence-based decision-making as an effective approach to selecting from the many choices people have to make regarding themselves and as individuals involved in the decision-making processes of their society.

PART III

Perspectives on Health Education

Introduction

Each paper in this section is concerned with some aspect of health education as perceived by the author of the paper. The opening paper by Dr. Sushila Nayar of the Mahatma Gandhi Institute of Medical Sciences in India reminds us forcefully of the importance of health education in rural areas in a developing country, but at the same time sees it against the background of all other socio-economic problems associated with poverty and political restraints. Jos Elstgeest emphasizes the realities of the classroom and warns of the difficulties in changing attitudes. Dolores Hernandez writes from the perspective of a biologist in "The Curriculum Guide to Teaching about Health", and incorporates in her contribution specific suggestions from the IUBS Commission on Biological Education on how health topics can be incorporated into biology teaching.

Quite different is Jane Rayne's contribution urging a positive approach to health, as opposed to concentration on medicine and disease (and incidentally she is the only author of the many advocating a positive approach who actually refers to the importance of rest). Saber Selim writes from the perspective of Egypt where children learn about bilharzia in the classroom and immediately afterwards start bathing in stagnant canal water: he urges the need to get the right emphasis in health education.

In Bangalore, there was a group much concerned with environmental aspects of health education and Winston King's contribution advocates that there should be a symbiotic relationship between biology, health education and environmental education as something vital to the well-being of all three.

Margaret Brumby follows this with a paper from the biological perspective advocating a re-definition of the boundaries of biology to take account of developments in biotechnology. Trefor Williams emphasizes the cultural and other factors which influence young people in addition to what they learn in school.

A very different perspective comes from Dr. H. V. Wyatt, who discusses whether Western medicine is compatible with traditional beliefs, asking

45

how they can be merged to ensure the best of each, instead of the worst, as he suspects is the case at the present time. Yet another different perspective comes from Dr. G. Stoltman and Dr. E. J. Wood in their contribution on the importance of cloning and biotechnology in combating disease. It was considered appropriate to include scientific contributions of this nature as it is likely that the cloning of cells and the use of biotechnology will have far-reaching implications for health and medicine in the future and will in due course affect education.

A final contribution in this section from U. N. Jajoo brings us back to the realities of the problems of developing countries with her contribution from the perspective of village life.

8

Health Education in Rural Areas

S. NAYAR

Mahatma Gandhi Institute of Medical Sciences, Sevagram, India

I had the good fortune to learn how to serve the health needs of our villages at the feet of Mahatma Gandhi. He was a votary of truth, and science seeks truth. He had no use for abstract theories. He was interested in the application of science to the betterment of the life of the masses living in our villages and in the slums of our cities.

I went to Sevagram in 1938 as a newly qualified medical graduate. The first task Gandhiji set me was to find out why there was a chain of cases of typhoid in the Ashram, one case after another. I went to observe the current patient and found that his excreta was being disposed of by burying it in a pit, without prior disinfection, not far from the Ashram well. A water sample from the well was sent to the Public Health Laboratory at Nagpur. It was found to be heavily contaminated with coliform organisms. A simple procedure of mixing bleaching powder (of which I had found a sackful in the Ashram) with the excreta of the patient before disposal, and of boiling the drinking water, broke the chain of typhoid cases.

The *first lesson* which I thus learnt was that Health Education is necessary and it is most effective when it is related to a real situation. No amount of abstract lectures and explanation about the infectiousness of the excreta of a typhoid patient, the need to disinfect it before disposal, and to boil drinking water could have carried conviction to the inmates of the Ashram, as this experience did.

After some time there was an outbreak of cholera in Sevagram. Gandhiji asked me to control it. I did it with the help of volunteers to whom I gave on-the-job training. The *second lesson* I learnt was that the volunteers could do a good job after short on-the-job training, but that active involvement of the family members and of the community leaders was also necessary if health work was to prove effective. We can only get such involvement if we cater for the needs they feel. In this case they were keen to have their sick treated and when we did this, they co-operated with us by getting themselves inoculated and by following instructions with regard to disinfection of the patients' excreta and soiled clothes.

In 1944 there was another epidemic of cholera in Wardha District and Gandhiji sent me from Poona to Wardha to control it. I was delighted to learn that our village of Sevagram had escaped the epidemic. A case of cholera came to our village from another village. The local leaders immediately responded. I saw that Gandhiji's insistence on my treating the patients in their own homes in the previous epidemic had brought the necessary awareness of their role and this had enabled them to protect their village from this latest epidemic.

The *third lesson* was that, if the community is sufficiently motivated, it will make the maximum use of the available health facilities and manage to protect its own health. In this case the villagers of Sevagram came to our dispensary and had the entire village inoculated, and took all the necessary precautions to protect themselves against cholera.

How to bring about this motivation is the question of questions. Health Education is the only answer. But what kind of health education will catch the imagination of villagers, how to impart it and how to get the instructions implemented are the questions which must be answered if any real impact is to be made.

This leads to the question: What is health? As mentioned in the introduction to this book, in our language the word for health is "Swasthaya". It is made of two parts – "Swa" means "self" and "Stha" means "stability". "Self Stability" or "Stability within Self" is perhaps the best definition of mental health. The importance of mental health for ensuring physical health needs no elaboration or explanation.

Our concern at the Mahatma Gandhi Institute in Sevagram has been the rural population of Wardha District. Health must be thought of in relation to the harmonious all-round development of every individual, physical, psychological and socio-economic. Individual health has to be seen in the context of the family and community health. No child is born an orphan and in the words of the 17th-century poet, John Donne: "No man is an island entire of itself". Every health care action has to be seen in the context of daily life and should have as its basis a close knowledge of the living conditions, the needs and aspirations of families and communities.

The dimensions of the concept of health have immensely broadened the field of health education. Health education in the wider context requires a certain attitude of mind and orientation of thought and action with the three main objectives: to inform, to motivate, and to set in motion the necessary action.

The Role of Women

Though there are more illiterate women than men, we find women learn more quickly and respond more readily and practically to information. They exercise great influence on the health habits of their families, as well as on their friends and neighbours. The sheer amount of work many of our village women have to get through leaves them little time to relax or learn new ideas. There may be a community radio in a village, but only the men can go and listen to it. Moreover, the All India Radio broadcasts generally contain information mainly of masculine interest. There is very little message about health education carried by the media, and its failure to reach women in the villages is regrettable. The role of women in promoting better health must be appreciated and arrangements made so that the message of health educators reaches them.

The ANMs (Auxiliary Nurses and Midwives) have played a significant role in the maternity and child health services, especially in the propagation of the norm of small families among village women. These female workers, who usually belong to indigenous stock, have a "much smaller distance" between the source of health education and the recipient and are therefore much better received. Word of mouth dissemination, especially in family planning, has been important to its success.

Health Education Experience and Social Service Camps

Village service is a unique part of the medical education imparted at the Mahatma Gandhi Institute of Medical Sciences. One important feature is the social service camp. In this camp the students actually stay for about a fortnight amongst the villagers in the selected village, becoming their friends, learning their health problems, assessing their socio-economic, socio-cultural and educational status. Probably it is the greatest opportunity for the MS BS medical students of learning community and family health care in the shortest time. It provides two weeks of intensive training in the community in the actual practice of community medicine and imparting health education.

The social service camp is a two-way method of providing learning opportunities, both to the students and to the villagers. They learn by exchanging views and experiences. An important aspect of the camp is free and frank discussion between students and staff with the villagers. Audio-visual aids are used as tools, an exhibition on health topics is arranged for the village and exhibits are explained by trainees and staff members. Actual demonstrations of the chlorination of wells, construction of soakage pits, kitchen gardens, compost pits and sanitary latrines are arranged. Every family is encouraged and helped in constructing these sanitary installations, and some of them actually do this.

The involvement of the community in the activities of the camp helps to achieve the goals. The experience of the camps brings out the importance of health education by living with those whom we wish to educate, even if only for a few days.

The Role of Village Health Committees

In the village Warud a health committee has been functioning for several years. It has seven members with the Sarpanch in the chair and the staff of the Department of Community Medicine at the Mahatma Gandhi Institute act as advisors to the committee. Solutions to health problems are sought through group discussions and the committee is the forum which aims at bringing about change in attitudes towards healthy living. Problems like the improvement in village sanitation through the provision of sanitary latrines, soak pits, kitchen gardens and some kind of drainage are being tackled with partial success.

In some villages health committees are set up with a selected primary school teacher as secretary and some school teachers have been able to achieve considerable success. A sister institution has tried health committees of women, involving the mothers-in-law, to promote pre-natal and post-natal care and infant care, along with family spacing. These have met with considerable success.

Village Health Insurance Scheme

The main purpose of a health insurance scheme is to create health consciousness and motivate families and rural communities to plan and provide for medical care in advance and to bring it within their means. The scheme has evolved over several years with the following objectives:

(a) to create awareness that health and medical care need to be provided for, even when there is no illness;

(b) to reach the rural poor, who often do not go for treatment because they cannot afford the expense;

(c) to provide promotive and preventive health care at the community level;

(d) to promote integrated development of the village with health care as the entry point (or to use as entry point any other need felt by the villagers, such as getting a loan, and then moving into health care and health education).

A recent health insurance scheme aims at payments in cash or kind by the villagers according to their economic status as determined by the village committees and then provides them with services according to their needs. This covers fifteen villages and there is a monthly visit by a mobile health team consisting of a doctor, an ANM and a social worker, while a village health guide is trained and posted in each village. During the visit by the team audio-visual health education programmes are undertaken; maternal and child health care is provided by holding clinics; mass immunization is undertaken; and care is provided for chronically ill patients. The insured family gets free hospital indoor services for all unexpected emergency illnesses. At present 65% of the families in the fifteen villages have been covered by the scheme and they mainly form the lower socio-economic strata.

What We Have Learnt

Our success in bringing about behavioural change in the community has been only partial. We have not been able to tackle the problems of village sanitation to the desirable level. However, we have learnt a number of lessons.

1. Medical services can be a good medium for developing contact with the people. To develop the concept of "Health for the people" and "by the people" in the true sense, an organized and informed community is necessary. It is difficult to get people's participation for health and medical problems on their own, as they are not the top priority for the village people. But medical and health work can certainly be complementary and can strengthen village co-operation where participation by the village has been sought and secured in other areas enjoying a higher priority with them, such as agriculture, employment, education, etc. Although health workers are poorly equipped to help with such problems, nevertheless attempts should be made by them to help villagers with what are their priority problems.

2. Socio-economic factors, poverty and the political framework today are the major constraints in the development of appropriate medical care, and for that matter for the all-round development of the village. These are matters about which nothing is taught during medical training and this requires immediate attention.

3. Most of the negative behaviour of the village people is their reaction to their environment. Inability on our part to understand their environment is chiefly responsible for the big communication gap between them and us.

4. Malnutrition is the most important health problem. The fight against this is in fact a fight against poverty and political and social injustice.

5. Medical field work is a very good educational tool to understand the limitations of medical science. The mystification of medicine and the role of socio-economic and political factors in causing health problems open up new areas of important field research.

6. Health education as a part of general education can lead to the betterment of life, based on better health of the community (physical, mental, social and economic).

7. The example set by respected leaders in their personal behaviour goes a long way in carrying conviction to the people and removing prejudice born of ignorance. For example, prejudice against leprosy patients and the fear of catching the infection among medical and paramedical personnel and lay public, was greatly reduced, if not removed, when Gandhiji started serving Perchure Shastri, an advanced case of lepromatous leprosy, with his own hands.

9

Children and Their Health

J. ELSTGEEST

Middelburg, The Netherlands

Health is not a matter of rules and regulations. The health of our children may be influenced by "do's" and by "don'ts", it does not consist of obedience. It consists in the well-being of each person, of each child, and that should be our point of departure when considering health education for young children. The aim of such education directs us to an intelligent attitude towards one's own well-being (care for oneself) and that of our community (care for each other).

Healthy attitudes are not acquired by being told about them. I once attended a lesson on bilharzia in a school which was situated on a hill surrounded by a very watery swamp. The teacher faithfully described the lifecycle of the parasite, how it travels and matures from human bowels into water, into snails, back into water and back into the human portal vein. His graphic visual aids left no doubts about some direputable habits. He summed up the symptoms and summarized the measures of preventing the disease. He could not have been more complete in his exposé. The children, well disposed to their teacher, listened with due attention and polite boredom, as usual, and dutifully scribbled the summary in their notebooks. Ninety per cent of these children suffered from the disease in various degrees of seriousness. No sooner was school over than the majority of those who lived nearby played and splashed with gay abandon in the snail-infested water until the sinking sun beckoned them home, the details of bilharzia blissfully tucked between the pages of their school exercise books.

Healthy attitudes do not develop from well meant propaganda and rightful or wishful thinking, however supportive this may be. No amount of lessons, books, pamphlets, posters or visiting experts in poorer stretches of tropical lands has ever left a trail of cleaner villages or healthier habits behind. Not by itself, that is. Listen to the following conversation:

Health educator: "What should be done to the drinking water in the village?"

Schoolboy:	"Drinking water should be filtered and boiled."
Health educator:	"Good. Why?"
Schoolboy:	"Because it is unsafe to drink unpurified water. It carries the germs of sickness."
Health educator:	"Splendid! And do you filter and boil your drinking water at home?" (big smile)
Schoolboy:	"No."
Health educator:	"But . . . do you not become sick then?" (big smile disappears)
Schoolboy:	"No."

This health educator obviously came from the "I shall tell them" school, and so did the boy, like the bilharzia children. At this school – who does not recognize it? – the children are given answers before they have had a chance to ask any questions. The questions will come from outside, from visiting health educators or from the makers of exams. Regurgitating these old answers previously given is the right response, because this assures you of good marks.

We have given children answers, but we kept the confidence to ourselves. We have given them memory, but we kept the thinking to ourselves. We have given them marks, but we kept the understanding to ourselves. We have given them questions in examinations, but we kept the ability to solve problems to ourselves. We have given them a health syllabus, but have we given them health?

Intelligent attitudes towards one's own health and well-being, as well as towards one's neighbours and surroundings, are built on the acquisition and the application of many concepts, all formed in relation to one's own experiences.

Sound application of concepts is further conditioned by the acquisition and exercise of such process skills as raising appropriate questions, finding patterns in observation, making sensible predictions or hypotheses, designing reliable experimentation, and seeking and selecting relevant information.

This seems a tall order for primary children, and so it is! Let us have no illusion about this: our primary children stand at the beginning of a long journey and we must have the patience to allow them to trudge along this route. They must do it themselves. We may support and guide them, but we cannot give them a lift. However, on their own level they can learn to solve problems, and thus exercise all these skills and abilities, provided we

(a) allow them the time they need;

(b) give them problems which they can handle;

[handwritten margin notes: "child's experiences more important"; "Ethos & environment more likely to influence"]

(c) give them materials to work with with which they are familiar, which they are confident to manipulate, and which are taken from their own (school) environment.

This implies carefully circumventing the misty multitudes of unrelated facts, rules, and ought-to's which come in many adult formulations on health education.

Taking the child, who is to accept responsibility toward his own well-being as well as that of others, as our point of departure places health education in a much broader context than the pure medico-biological connotation it is so often given. It becomes an integral aspect of the conscious intervention we exert on a child's development which we call education. Naturally, the stage of development of a primary school child puts restrictions on the ambitions we have with regard to health education, and we should be very much aware of that. However, the development process is continuous and some insight in the process of intellectual and affective development in young children will serve the teacher in discerning children's capabilities. Which next step have they reached? Seeing health education as a contribution to people's care for their own well-being and that of others, we may distinguish the following desirabilities:

– Healthy habits
– Healthy concepts
– Healthy attitudes
– Healthy judgement and decision-making.

The sequence given here is not arbitrary. Although there is not a chronological order, there is a kind of sequential order in the sense that one can conceive these desired achievements as recurring steps in an upward spiral. Each step is an enhancement of those following and a confirmation or reinforcement of the previous one.

Healthy Habits

Habits are acquired by doing things consistently and are maintained in the same way. The maintenance of a desirable habit may be reinforced by reminders: external ones given by the authoritative adult educator, or internal reminders originating from insight and sound judgement.

In the early stages of development children follow rules and commands in a rather matter-of-fact way. Behaviour is very much externally controlled, and motivated by fear of punishment or desire for praise and reward. This is the beginning of many household virtues and habits of cleanliness, and safety: washing hands, brushing teeth, combing hair, tucking in shirt-tails, flushing the toilet, staying away from water and highways, leaving matches alone. No amount of explanatory talk improves on the simple command: "do" or "don't". Without going into further details of desired behaviour, we can say that home and school play a common role here: just get things done properly and keep it so; remind when forgetfulness threatens to upset the established order. This is a necessary beginning of healthy habit formation commanded by plain common sense.

However, the reminding may increasingly refer to the growing understanding of the children with regard to their own self, and the way things work. In other words, the how and the why of their desired behaviour is related to acquired concepts, adopted attitudes and emerging judgement.

Concepts

Children make a long journey through their environment, their world, in which they have countless encounters with things, with forces, and events, with creatures great and small, plants, insects, situations, dangers, frights, illnesses, feasts, and sometimes disasters. All these experiences form the basis of their knowledge and their responsive understanding of their world. Making sense of it all and adjusting oneself in it is a natural ability of each child, but which can be greatly enhanced by thoughtful education. And is this not a natural basis for general well-being which is the essence of good health? Primary science education becomes good health education not by selecting specific subject matter from a pool of some adult's pet conceptions, but by helping children to come to terms with their environment which starts right within themselves.

Not very long ago I saw infants, five-year-olds, sprawled around the floor of their classroom around a big drawing of a human shape. They were drawing where exactly they thought they had experienced ills and sicknesses. They were locating various pains and disorders which they had just talked about in connection with the absence of a few sick classmates. The result of this activity was a pretty accurate map of children's ills which they perfectly understood.

A thorough study of "the human body" by primary children is possible only if they use their own (and each other's) body as a source of information. Apart from measuring and comparing wholes and parts, they can experiment with their skin and sensitive spots on it; they can observe and feel heads and limbs, they can experiment with heartbeats; they can observe, feel and compare scalp and limbs, teeth and toes; they can feel and map bones and joints, and they can play with muscles and reflexes, with senses and responses. These activities often lead to questions about insides and workings which escape direct observation. Interest is kindled. Questions are a sure sign that they want to know. Besides, experiencing your own body in this "scholarly" way provides a frame of reference for the clarification and acceptance of even the most obnoxious daily duties and habits of healthy maintenance.

The study of animals and plants in an equally active and involved way, and the influence on their behaviour of situational circumstances (controlled by the children or observed in nature) will provide them with the means to tie separate concepts together into patterns of relationships, and thus of understanding. This active involvement in woes and whims of fellow living creatures increases their feeling of mastery which, too, is a pillar supporting sound healthy behaviour.

If specific "topics of health" are to be introduced, then a selection of these must be related to the experience of the children: to their scientific work in the classroom, to the habits they have already adopted and intelligently accepted, to the diseases which occur in their own neighbourhood or to dangers lurking in their own environment.

Yet we must be careful. I have seen children, and not just a few, who firmly believe that the housefly (and some even remembered "Musca domestica") is an enormous monster who collects dirt on huge hairy legs by walking up and down dungheaps, after which it deliberately steps on the food of people and leaves filthy footprints behind.

The huge "visual aids" used to help understanding showed the fly in such unfamiliar proportions that the relation with the irksome pests buzzing about their ears was not clear to these children.

A promising teacher, strictly adhering to his health and hygiene syllabus, taught his class about "How to keep the compound clean". On the blackboard appeared the list of types of garbage together with the rules on how to dispose of them. The syllabus required practical experience so the teacher really made a job of it partly, perhaps, because he was being inspected. He had carefully littered the school compound with the required kinds of trash. When the children were taken outside to learn their lesson practically in their familiar surroundings, he let them burn the scattered pieces of paper, he made them dig pits for the old tins and broken bottles and, finally, the children collected the droppings of chickens and goats in their hands and disposed of these among the flowerbeds. Never had that school compound been cleaned so thoroughly. Teacher and children returned to the classroom to write the summary of the lesson in their notebooks. Nobody, including the teacher, ever thought of first going and washing hands . . . But then, the washing of hands sits somewhere else in the syllabus and will be dealt with in its proper time. Or could this be a matter of attitude?

Attitudes

This is not the place to start a discussion on the definition of "attitude". I use the word here in the rather popular sense of: "what you think of . . ." or "the way you feel about . . ." an object, an event, or a situation. Viewed from the side of the person concerned, "thinking of" and "feeling about" constitute a two-legged, cognitive and effective, basis for a certain (pre)disposition to (re)act in a certain way to that object, event, or situation.

The "thinking of" and the "feeling about" are, of course, closely related to the experiences on which one's concepts and conceptual schemes are built and correlated, but not alone. Attitudes towards one's own well-being (health) are also closely related to "well feeling", a disposition of harmony with oneself and the world. This in turn is the beginning of the acceptance of a responsibility towards the well-being of one's neighbour.

The care which children more or less consciously develop and exercise towards themselves, that is, their own health and harmony, serves as an example for the care they develop and exercise towards others. Only in this context do measures for public health, safety rules, traffic codes, health warnings, and related appeals for social behaviour, make sense to children. When a rule makes sense, it is accepted as a matter of course, and no longer obeyed out of fear.

A basic attitude which is always desirable in the pursuit of science, and thus an objective of good science education, is the willingness to ask the right question at the right time, together with the willingness to search for an honest answer, and the willingness to accept the consequences of action demanded by this honest answer. And this leads us to judgement and decision-making.

Judgement and Decision-making

An ever recurring step in the process which spirals up to good health as a personal achievement, rather than as a treatise on paper, is the making of sound judgement concerning action to be taken in one's own personal life, with regard to others or to the benefit of the whole community. This judgement sanctions such simple common habits as washing hands before meals and brushing teeth after. It can also lead to decisions to undergo unpleasant treatment or surgery, or giving up bad habits. Sound judgement, too, sanctions such public health measures as draining infested swamps, or passing anti-drug laws.

Sound judgement is the only guarantee for preventive measures which depend on the co-operation of the populace to be successful and effective. For example: if people are to prevent getting bilharzia by not bathing in infected water (and is this not a simple and straightforward measure of prevention?), it is insufficient merely to tell them this. People who for the first, for the second or indeed for the third time undergo the very unpleasant cure of twelve nasty injections on twelve consecutive days are told how to prevent bilharzia. Children in schools are all told about the treacherous ways of the parasite which causes the disease. Doctors and nurses explain it to their patients, and community centres display posters and warnings. People are well informed, yet it looks as if this information has fallen on stony ground, remaining dead and sterile. As long as people do not ask themselves: "How does bilharzia come about?" and "What can I do to prevent getting it?", they will not attempt to answer such questions. As long as they are not aware of the problem, they will not understand the answer when it is given to them. People will only understand why the preventive measures are necessary, and act accordingly, if they can think as scientists. This means that they must be able to reason out for themselves the relation between cause and effect. In other words, they must be able to apply the process of science to the information given to them. Even without knowing all the medical and zoological details, people should be able to appreciate that there is a relationship between their own actions and the occurrence of a disease like bilharzia. They will only take preventive measures if they make an autonomous decision to do so.

It is, therefore, essential that all citizens are educated to make intelligent decisions based on an understanding of their environment, sustained by an inquiring mind, guided by critical appraisal of truth and values, and reinforced by the ability to identify and solve problems which arise from the needs within this environment.

This reduces a vast mass of educational objectives to three essentials: independent thinking, wise decision-making and the confidence to rely on these qualities in the environmental setting in which one finds oneself.

Primary children find themselves in a primary setting. They can do primary science, and our health-educational objectives should reflect this primary reality.

10

A Curriculum Guide to Teaching about Health

D. F. HERNANDEZ
University of the Philippines

This contribution is based on a paper previously written for a booklet on Health Education and Biology Teaching produced under the auspices of the Commission for Biological Education of the International Union of Biological Sciences and Unesco.

Health education is derived from a number of sources. For this reason it is important to bear in mind the following points when planning programmes of health education in the school curriculum:

Health education in schools cannot be a substitute for the training of professional public health adults for work in the community.

Health education in school is part of a larger educational programme aimed at delivering health care and services to the population as a whole. It is therefore important that teachers are aware of community health programmes and services so that duplication is avoided and co-ordination is enhanced.

In planning a programme of school health education it is important to ensure that the school itself is a safe and healthy environment for young people and that health services are available to the extent that the school system is able to afford them.

Health education may be included in several subjects, for example biology, physical education, home economics, domestic science, general science. Rarely is health education taught as a separate subject. This implies that to have an effective health education programme there must be co-ordination among all teachers who incorporate health education in their courses.

Selection of content relating to the universal concepts of health must be orientated to local conditions in the students' immediate environment, their community and their country.

Where health education is part of the biology curriculum, there should be balance and harmony between health topics and biological concepts. The basic concepts of biology should not be lost because of the health aspects. It is suggested that in a science or biology curriculum which is health orientated, there should be greater coverage of basic health principles at the elementary level, whilst biology as a discipline should have greater prominence at the secondary level of education.

A Model for Teaching Health Education Through Biology

The figure opposite depicts a possible overall scheme for relating biology teaching to health education. It is based on two central themes.

First, that there should be a core of teaching based on principles drawn from elementary biology and/or integrated science courses, which develop into a curriculum consisting of such topics as nutrition, disease and immunization, environmental health and first aid. From this in turn are established the essential principles of preventive medicine and primary health care.

Secondly, that as this curriculum unfolds during the school life of a student, there should be an increasing emphasis on topics of increasing socio-biological complexity, from aspects of personal health to the wider health problems involved in population studies and conservation. In parallel to this, there should also be an increasing emphasis on aspects of health care from the simple to the more complex, that is, from home health to community health and so to national health programmes.

Student-centred Objectives

A scheme such as the one just outlined only provides a frame-work for a curriculum. The next step is to determine what specific attributes one would wish students to have acquired at the end of their studies. The following list of objectives has been developed as a consensus of views from several countries.

1. Develop an ability to discriminate between fact and opinion in information related to health.
2. Acquire knowledge of body systems and functions with an understanding that growth and development of these systems follow a predictable pattern with many normal variations, producing unique individuals.
3. Develop an understanding of the relationship between physical and emotional (mental) well-being.
4. Develop an understanding of the need for proper nutrition.
5. Develop the skills necessary for physical fitness.

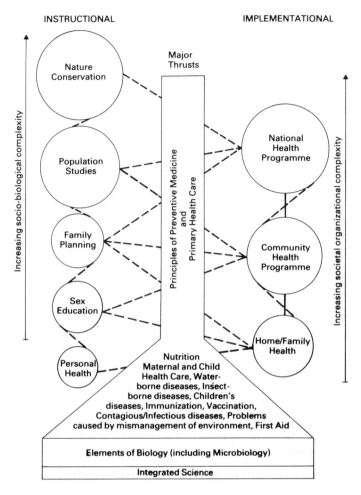

INSTRUCTIONAL — IMPLEMENTATIONAL

Increasing socio-biological complexity

Increasing societal organizational complexity

Nature Conservation

Population Studies

Family Planning

Sex Education

Personal Health

Major Thrusts

Principles of Preventive Medicine and Primary Health Care

National Health Programme

Community Health Programme

Home/Family Health

Nutrition Maternal and Child Health Care, Water-borne diseases, Insect-borne diseases, Children's diseases, Immunization, Vaccination, Contagious/Infectious diseases, Problems caused by mismanagement of environment, First Aid

Elements of Biology (including Microbiology)

Integrated Science

6. Develop an awareness of the relationship between human beings and the natural and social environments.

7. Develop a body of knowledge about the causative agents and preventive measures relative to the common communicable diseases in the environment, and develop positive behaviours and attitudes regarding the control of such diseases.

8. Develop responsible behaviours and attitudes relative to sanitation in the home and community.

9. Develop an ability to make responsible decisions about alcohol, tobacco and other drugs.

10. Develop an understanding of the role of being an effective parent and the role of the family in contemporary society.

11. Develop an ability to make informed decisions concerned with sexuality.

12. Develop responsible attitudes towards family planning in consonance with a country's population programme.

13. Acquire knowledge of the range of vocational opportunities in health and allied fields.

Fitting the Teaching of Health Topics into Biology Syllabuses

In the following two tables are listed, in the left-hand column, biological topics to be found in syllabuses of elementary and secondary schools respectively in several countries. Opposite each topic are suggested health topics which can be linked to them, suggested activities through which the topics can be taught and, in the fourth column, the skills and attitudes which would be developed with the activities.

The tables are intended as a resource that teachers can use to plan their own curriculum using the objectives listed above as a guide. It is important that curricula be worked out in detail at the local level. It is only there that final decisions can be made regarding specific topics to be included in teaching. For example, the local foods and their nutritive values, local diseases, local health problems and health concerns of young people must be considered in determining the day-to-day learning experiences of the curriculum.

The scheme will help remind teachers to select health topics that relate to major biological themes or concepts in their own syllabus, provide experiences that involve students in their own learning, and attend to the skills and attitudes that can be developed as a result of the knowledge and experiences provided in the curriculum.

Curriculum Map for the Elementary Level

Biological Topics	Suggested Health Topics	Suggested Activities	Skills and Attitudes
Useful plants and animals	Common plants in the local environment that serve as food sources for man/ animal, have medicinal value, have nutritional value Useful animals in the local environment that serve as food sources; nutritive value of animal products	Field trip to: market (vegetable, fruit, meat and fish, dairy products sections); orchards, vegetable gardens; medicinal plant gardens Field trip to slaughterhouse or a report on how animals are prepared for the consumer, the sanitary measures taken Encourage pupils to identify medicinal plants from common vegetation about them. Demonstrate how to prepare and use herbal medicine properly Encourage pupils to have a school medicinal garden	Awareness of the role of traditional (herbal) medicine as part of the overall health delivery system Valuing the need for sanitation regulations in markets, slaughterhouses and other places where food is prepared
The sense organs – how we get to know about the world	Care of the senses of sight, hearing and balance, touch, taste Care of the teeth: primary teeth and permanent teeth	Do some simple experiments on: taste (identify parts of the tongue sensitive to sweet, sour, bitter tastes) touch (guessing an object by using only the sense of touch) sight – how much can you see with one eye? Discuss some simple do's and don't's in regard to maintaining healthy eyes, ears, teeth	Awareness that disabilities in the senses e.g., sight and hearing, can affect learning Valuing the importance of healthy sense organs
The other body systems muscular skeletal digestive	Keeping the body systems healthy Importance of nutrition for health	Demonstrate/discuss appropriate health habits (relative to muscles, bones, digestion, circulation, etc.) Discuss common ailments related to the body systems Discuss physical aspects of emotion (organs in the body that respond to fear, sadness, etc.)	Practise health habits relating to the body systems Develop awareness of the importance of mental, emotional physical health

Biological Topics	Suggested Health Topics	Suggested Activities	Skills and Attitudes
circulatory respiratory excretory		Identify foods that contribute to the healthy condition of the systems Observe organs, tissues of the different systems in animals (obtained from a meat market) Identify non-conventional food sources available in the community Demonstrate proper ways of preparing and cooking vegetables to retain nutrients	Develop awareness of the importance of having a balanced diet Develop awareness of existing sources of inexpensive but nutritious foods
Micro-organisms, immunology	Common communicable diseases, their prevention Immune systems of the body Guarding against harmful microbes by: a healthy body building up resistance avoiding microbes, or keeping microbes away from the body	Do some experiments to demonstrate presence of microbes on the hands, in the air, water Observe visuals on spread of common communicable diseases in the country Discuss ways of preventing common communicable diseases Survey the class for leading diseases occurring in their families Discuss body defences Identify foods that help make the body strong Read the story of Pasteur Look at the organisms in a drop of pond water	Develop proper attitudes towards prevention of diseases through appropriate health habits Awareness that medicines should be taken with caution or under prescription of the doctor
Human activity and life Living things have similar needs in any environment: food, water shelter, protection against extremes	The home and school environment cleanliness at home and school and their surroundings health habits: (a) body parts – hair,	Role-playing on critical incidents involving interpersonal relations Use posters to demonstrate good health habits, personal hygiene Identify the community's needs relative to sources of food and water supply	Develop awareness of man's interdependence with his natural and physical environment Develop preference for an environment that is aesthetic and sanitary

...creation/construction preservation of objects that enhance a beautiful sanitary environment

Active involvement in physical fitness programmes offered in the school/community

Develop awareness of and practice of proper sanitation in the home, school and community

...temperature, etc. There are different kinds of environment each with characteristic features and life

Living things and the environment interchange matter and energy; some plants and animals: what they take from the environment and what they give to the environment

Cycles in nature

...skin, teeth, nails, individual or personal hygiene
(b) clothing
(c) meal time
(d) sleep and rest
(e) food and drink
(f) exercise and leisure
(g) sense organs
(h) safety precautions

The social environment; interpersonal relations with family, friends, neighbours

The physical environment: sanitation at home, in school, in the community providing safe drinking water, sanitary garbage and waste disposal

Brief lectures, discussions on sex education topics as included in the school curriculum. This could link up with the foregoing topic on growth

Demonstration of first aid procedures for emergencies of common occurrence in the school/community

Describe changes in the community; their impact on health conditions. Use visuals

Initiate a conservation project

Discuss with illustrations the benefits of exercise to the human body. Give the rationale from a biological viewpoint of some exercises/games for physical fitness (co-ordinate with the physical education instructor)

Encourage participation in physical fitness programmes

The environment is in constant change. Noting changes in the community (within the child's experience)

Man as a major agent of change in the environment

First aid (e.g., poisoning, wounds, animal and insect bites, drowning, fainting, shock, etc.)

Growing up mentally, physically, socially

Signs of health and illness

Sex education and family planning; infant care and nutrition; maternal care

Biological Topics	Suggested Health Topics	Suggested Activities	Skills and Attitudes
	Desirable and undesirable changes in the environment from the viewpoint of improved health conditions in the community; sources of pollution of air, water, soil in the community Physical fitness		
The commonly used drugs caffeine (coffee, tea, cocoa, cola drinks) nicotine (tobacco) alcohol the most commonly used drugs for this age group in the community	Nutrition and coffee, tea and carbonated drinks Effect of alcoholic beverages on body systems Tobacco and smoking: effect on the respiratory system General and overall effect of abused drugs on the body systems	Examine nutritive value of common drinks Examine advertisements: what effect do they have on the reader?	Develop awareness of the uses of drugs in medication, and their irresponsible use by individuals Develop awareness of the need for caution in the use of abused drugs and drugs sold "over-the-counter"

Curriculum Map for the Secondary Level

Biological Topics	Suggested Health Topics	Suggested Activities	Skills and Attitudes
Cell structure and functions Molecules of life	Effects of alcohol, drugs, tobacco on cells Possible physical effects of excessive use of alcohol over long period of time Effects of alcohol abuse and alcoholism on the family, the community, the person's ability to function The role of drugs in the prevention and control of disease and pain Effect of chemical and environmental mutagens on the cell e.g., heavy metals, pesticides and insecticides, radiation and food additives	Have the students observe cells of various types under the microscope, both live and dead cells Collect materials from the Heart Center, Lung Center, Drug and Narcotics Division or other similar organizations and make an informative exhibit relative to health concepts studied Have the students identify the organs and systems of the body that are most affected by excessive use of alcohol. Describe how these organs are affected and what it means to the overall health of the individual Have the students bring to class magazine and newspaper ads on alcoholic beverages; have them describe TV ads too. Have them identify misleading statements/illustrations, and discuss how they think these ads would influence young people's attitudes Invite a doctor to speak on medical uses of drugs on: the nervous system, cardiovascular system, gastrointestinal system, the blood, the endocrine system	Develop a positive attitude towards health protection of the individual and family by safeguarding health, by supporting health plans Be aware of the extent of drug dependency in the age group and its effects on the person Be involved in programmes designed to alleviate drug abuse, alcoholism Recognize the importance of drugs in medicine Recognize that there is existing information on recommended limits to the use of food additives, heavy metals, radiation, pesticides and insecticides and develop a sense of responsibility for safeguarding health relative to the application of such information

Biological Topics	Suggested Health Topics	Suggested Activities	Skills and Attitudes
Life activities of living organisms	Common ailments associated with: the heart and circulation respiratory system the liver and the kidney digestive system nervous system excretory system endocrine system	Demonstrate exercises that stimulate circulation; good health practices relating to the different systems	Develop first aid skills to preserve life/meet emergencies
Body structure and functions of the various systems of the body that maintain life		Demonstrate first aid methods for artificial respiration; wounds involving large blood vessels; food poisoning; other emergencies that commonly occur in the school/community	Develop respect for life Develop awareness of effects of taking in spoiled food
		Have the students list "risk" factors in heart disease	Recognize the dangers of smoking to health
		Have the students interview and report on what a doctor listens to with a stethoscope	Develop skills in decision-making
	Ways of keeping healthy	Invite a doctor to talk about disorders of the mind and the nervous system	Realize the importance of caring for the heart and the circulatory system
	the various body functions that maintain life	List the most common respiratory diseases in the school/ community; have students collect data on the prevalence of these diseases in the community. Have students collect materials on the causative agents and preventive measures against these diseases	Develop skills in first aid
	The effect of proper nutrition on the different organ systems to attain homeostasis	Have students examine beef or sheep lungs and trachea at organ and tissue level	
	Bacterial and viral respiratory diseases and those of congenital origin	Discuss effects of smoking on respiratory system	
	Coronary heart disease	Use case histories to have students find clues whether the individuals described are at high or low risks of coronary heart disease. Have them discuss what could be done to lower the risk	
	Common accidents involving the musculoskeletal system in this age group (use quantitative data, i.e., accident statistics if possible)	Invite medical doctor/s to talk on the prevalence of health disease in the population	
		Have students practise first aid techniques after they have been exposed to various lessons involving first aid. The practice sessions should include decision-making as to what first aid treatment is to be given and in what order	
		Participation in school/community fitness programmes	
		Invite a doctor, school counsellor/psychologist to talk on ways of coping with stress	

Biological Topics	Suggested Health Topics	Suggested Activities	Skills and Attitudes
	Relationship of the skeletal and muscular systems to body movement and posture Coping with stress		
Classification of living organisms beneficial and harmful organisms: bacteria viruses, yeasts and moulds, amoeba, worms	Microorganisms and diseases Common communicable diseases in the country, the community Helping the body resist harmful microorganisms What the individual can do to keep the body functioning well Identify the parasites common among children of the community Collect and demonstrate use of medicinal plants as dewormers Life cycles of organisms that are parasitic to man; which stage is most dangerous to its human host	Have students prepare a report on the 10 most common causes of death and morbidity in the community. What type of disease are most of them? (communicable or non-communicable) Invite doctor/s and a community health worker to talk about specific diseases common in the community, status of health in the community Discuss preventive measures relative to the most common diseases in the community Have students examine prepared slides of disease-producing bacteria Have the students grow colonies of bacteria, mould yeasts Study types of parasitic worms; identify diseased meat and fish as possible sources of parasites	Develop a positive attitude towards prevention of diseases as practised by the individual Develop a sense of responsibility for maintenance of healthy conditions in one's community Develop health habits to keep one's body fit Develop preference for disease prevention and control to treatment or rehabilitation

Biological Topics	Suggested Health Topics	Suggested Activities	Skills and Attitudes
Living organisms need food	Nutrients needed by the body	Demonstrate proper eating habits; preparing food correctly	Develop skills in preparing food properly, checking one's own daily food requirements
food and nutrition	How much energy the body needs	Check one's diet for nutrient values	
digestion of nutrients	Food for energy, growth, regulation of the body's work	Relate nutrition to work productivity; under-nutrition effects on growth and development (use local data)	Develop familiarity with local food attitudes and beliefs, examining these in the light of health practices and knowledge
	Proper preparation of food	Show students how to calculate their daily food intake by looking up the number of calories and the quantities of nutrients associated with each food. Have them compare with the daily expenditure intake based on results, they plan what they should do	
	Eating habits	Give reasons for good health practices like making meal times pleasant, relaxing before meals when worried or under a strain, cooking starchy foods thoroughly, etc.	Develop decision-making skills
	Food and dental care	Invite a resource person to talk about the world's food supply and demand	Develop tolerance towards food preferences of population subgroups
	Energy from food	Calculate how many calories you take in a day; compare with the requirement for your age and weight (use local data). Compare the average intake of the girls vs. the boys in your class	Become aware of sociocultural factors that affect nutrition patterns in a population
	Food additives and health	Prepare a report on alternative sources of protein to those traditionally used	Become aware of effects of nutrition deficiencies on work efficiency
		Have the students read various food labels and identify food additives in them including nitrates and nitrites; identify also the nutrients present in the packaged food	Develop preference for nutritional fact over food fads
		Have students list all additives found in packaged food labels and identify what these do to the body	Develop skills in evaluating facts and information
		Have students read the labels for economy. Show how to calculate how much nutrient the consumer gets per unit of cost (per dollar, peso, etc.)	Develop skills in
		Have the students conduct a survey of food choices in their own class. Have them evaluate these choices from the viewpoint of nutrition	

Biological Topics	Suggested Health Topics	Suggested Activities	Skills and Attitudes
Reproduction in man human reproductive system; glands important in reproduction; menstrual cycle Development and growth Family planning Methods of birth control	Hormones in puberty and pregnancy Sex differences and energy needs Sex glands and body development Sex education Education for parenthood, preconception health and family planning, prenatal, delivery and postnatal maternal health; infant and child health child rearing interpersonal relationships home management Prenatal care Care of infants Growing old and degenerative diseases Sexually transmitted diseases	Survey family size in the community Prepare reports on population and resource forecast for the next two decades. Discuss implications Provide facts to replace myths students have about impregnation, VD, birth control, homosexuality and other areas of concern Examine methods of contraception in relation to availability, effectiveness and possible side effects Discuss psychological factors in general by having students submit their questions in written form. These can then be organized by topic. Resource persons may be invited for questions needing more specialized/complex answers Collect beliefs on pregnancy and child care; discuss/clarify implications Invite an appropriate resource person to help clarify issues related to this topic Discuss problems of population control; responsible parenthood	locating reliable information Develop positive attitudes toward: population control infant, child and maternal care Development of desirable sexual attitudes and behaviour including acceptance of heterosexual roles as boys and girls Develop ability to make informed decisions in the area of sexuality
Heredity Genetic engineering	Misconceptions about genetic health Genetic disorders; their causes, transmission in the population;	Secure information from the local hospital/s about the most frequently occurring birth defects; what are some of the dominant genetic diseases in the population?	To appreciate the significance of genetic health as an urgent health matter Recognize the role

Biological Topics	Suggested Health Topics	Suggested Activities	Skills and Attitudes
	prevention and/or rehabilitation		played by both the genes and the environment in shaping the individual
	Influence on health of: expanding population, poverty, social implications of these factors		
Man and his environment	Guarding community health	Have the students look up community and national health regulations and report on this topic	Develop positive attitudes to community sanitation
Man's activities and their impact on the environment	public water supply	Analyse (make a bacterial count of) the school or community water supply. Have students draw inferences about their observations	Develop awareness and commitment towards maintaining the environment as a healthful and aesthetic place for man's habitation
waste disposal	public waste disposal	Get data regarding pollution from the National Pollution Council or similar agency. Discuss implications of the data to the health of the community	
use of chemicals	other health services	Observe pollution count index in strategic places. Discuss implications to health and remedial measures that may be undertaken	
polluting the air	The citizen's role in keeping the home and community sanitary	Have the students find out how their community disposes of waste. Let them evaluate it in terms of standards of sanitation	
illegal logging	The citizen's role in minimizing pollution of:	Have the students find out whether the river/stream/pond water in the community is polluted; if so how heavily polluted it is, using simple BOD techniques. Visit a polluted body of water, identify evidence of hastened eutrophication. Have students discuss possible causes of eutrophication and the implications to water organisms	
noise pollution	air	Locate local studies on pollution. Have the students summarize the findings and discuss implications relative to health	
	water	Have some students report on the use of agricultural pesticides and insecticides, implications to health and pollution, the benefits derived from their use. Have a general discussion	
	land		
	noise		
	Practices by which man destroys the quality of the environment		

Biological Topics	Suggested Health Topics	Suggested Activities	Skills and Attitudes
		on what they would do if they were farmers Perform activities or experiments on waste utilization or recycling of materials	
Medicine, alcohol, drugs and tobacco	Alcohol and health Drug education Smoking and health	Discuss how excessive amounts of alcohol affect one's ability to function Discuss how the environment can influence a person's decision on the use or nonuse of alcohol Identify the physical, social and emotional risks involved in alcohol abuse Analyse the effects of advertising on a person's decision to drink or nor to drink Describe immediate effects of tobacco smoke on the body Evaluate the effects of tobacco advertisement on smoking behaviour Have the students discuss the rights of nonsmokers to unpolluted air Identify various psychological and sociological causes of drug abuse; use case studies from drug rehabilitation centres Invite a doctor, counsellor to talk on the physical, psychological and social effects of drug abuse Describe the role of drugs in the prevention and control of disease and pain. Invite a knowledgeable resource person like a pharmacist or doctor	Be aware of responsible alternative behaviours Develop the ability to make responsible decisions about alcohol, drugs, and tobacco

11

Communicating the Principles of Health

J. RAYNE
London, UK

> "One of the first duties of the physician is to educate people not to take medicine"
> (Sir William Osler)

It is a fairly well-known fact, but not by any means widely enough known, that the graveyards and hospitals of the world are full of people who would not be there had they been better educated with regard to their own health. What is worse is the fact that the number of such poorly educated people is not decreasing. This is something that the leaders of education in the world can do something about as health education should have an essential place in all schools. Health education cannot be left to the doctors as they simply do not have the time. Even those training medical students usually have to limit their teaching to symptoms and cures, rather than how to prevent the patient getting the symptoms in the first place. The governments of the world tend to spend money on equipment and drugs, but little by comparison on educating children about how to keep healthy in the first place. Health education programmes, covering every aspect of keeping healthy and suited to the needs of each country, should be as important a subject within the school curriculum as science or mathematics.

Ingredients of Health

Instead of the concentration on symptoms and cures, there are much more fundamental questions which need to be asked when there are signs of ill-health.

What do you eat?
What do you drink?
What exercise do you take?
What rest do you take?
What is your life like at home – stressful or peaceful?

What is your environment like?
What are your relationships with other people like?
What do you believe in?

It is the importance of the issues raised in questions like these which needs to be communicated through health education.

There are certain factors appertaining to each of the above questions which apply to people whatever country they live in.

(a) Food

The importance of a balanced diet has been stressed repeatedly in this book as also in the companion volume on Food and Agriculture. In some countries there are the problems of over-eating or the eating of foods which put great strains on the body to digest and expel. In others there is the eating of inappropriate foods, leading to a lack of balance. Nutritional education has to begin in schools as the parents of today are often as badly informed as their children.

(b) Drink

In so many countries, water is not suitable to drink and must be boiled. It is also important that there should be an awareness of the dangers of drinking large quantities of coffee, tea, cocoa, cola drinks and soft drinks. Health education should not neglect reference to alcoholic drinks.

(c) Exercise

Exercise is vital in order to maintain a healthy body and mind. But it is only one factor in a total programme. It is no good eating badly or drinking the wrong fluids (which are strains on the body) and then going out jogging five hours a day. The body simply cannot cope with the stress. Exercise must be part of a healthy living plan. Walking, swimming and cycling help the circulation just as much as jogging and aerobics. The body needs exercise every day to relax and get rid of tension as well as to oxygenate the blood adequately. It can be as little as running up and down stairs twice a day or as much as walking a couple of miles to work or school. Most children have no problems at all in this area, just playing with each other gives them plenty of exercise. But they have to become aware of the dangers in adult life of sitting at work all day.

(d) Rest

The importance of rest is never touched on by the majority of parents and schools. Too many times a major breakdown in health is caused by exhaustion which the patient or doctor does not recognize as such. One of the major causes of heart disease is exhaustion and this is only just beginning to be recognized by the medical profession. People struggling to overcome great difficulties in their lives, be they financial, emotional or physical, can push themselves over the limit of normal fatigue. At this point, body and mind cannot take the rest which is needed. Without proper sleep, the sufferers begin a downward spiral into exhaustion, each day pushing themselves further until a major breakdown occurs. This is not always realized by the doctors, whose training ought to include more about the healthy body as well as how to treat the diseased one. Health education at school level should certainly emphasize the importance of sleep and rest.

(e) Hygiene

The natural environment plays a very large part in this, but it must also be remembered that the social environment has an important role in producing good habits and that parents and teachers have to give examples of hygienic living themselves. Hygiene is best taught to children in the form of a routine in order to create habits – for example, cleaning teeth, toilet training, washing hands, throwing rubbish in suitable containers, bathing, etc. Even in a filthy or contaminated environment, people can achieve health by means of enforced hygienic effort.

(f) Social Relationships

The human body and mind need to make contact with other human beings in order to grow healthily. It is vitally important for children to have physical as well as emotional and mental contact with their parents. A genuine hug, a stroke of the hair, the holding of a hand can go a lot further to convince a child that he or she is loved than many a word spoken without much feeling. Grown-ups need such contacts as well. John Lennon was being profound when he said "All you need is love". We are all so often afraid to give or ask support of each other and even more afraid to show our feelings. But without emotional contact, people very soon lose confidence in life and fall sick.

(g) Spiritual Well-being

Beyond material aspects and social relationships, there is always the question of what is beyond. It is a question of transcendence which many people answer in a specific religious way. For such people belief in a transcendent force leads to final happiness and a spiritual well-being. Such spiritual well-being can certainly not be produced by education, however it can be anticipated by the teacher.

Conclusion

In the 1980s the world is full of technological, chemical and emotional dangers for human beings and they must be taught how to deal with these dangers and how to live a healthy life in spite of them. However marvellous the new discoveries of the medical and pharmaceutical world, many have lost sight of the very basic reasons why people become unhealthy.

If the present generation of children were truly and realistically educated as to the basic needs required by the body and the mind in order to be healthy, the future generations of doctors, pharmacists, nurses, scientists and healers in general would ensure that the hospitals and graveyards of the world were more filled with old people ending or having ended a normal span of life. The need is education to communicate the principles of health.

12

Getting the Right Emphasis in Health Education

M. SELIM

Cairo, Egypt

Biology is the school subject most related to health. Since good health is so vital to the quality of life, one would expect it to be an important part of the core of biology education, especially at the level of general education. Unfortunately this is not the case in Egypt.

Biology Education in Egypt

In primary schools there is a combined science course called "Science and Health". This deals with some aspects of health, for example, body systems, diseases, parasites, nutrition and so on. But the way these topics are taught amounts in most cases to preaching, and stresses memorization. Its effect on improving the health of youngsters is very limited.

At the lower secondary stage (grades 7–9) the General Science which is studied is not integrated in any way, but includes separate units of physics, chemistry and biology. There is a biology unit for every year of these 3 years.

At the upper secondary stage (grades 10–12) all students do a biology course of two hours a week in grade 10. In grades 11 and 12, science students will do a course of three hours a week, while arts students do no biology at all.

At the tertiary level, biology is offered in special colleges, such as scientific, agricultural, medical and teachers' colleges.

The Content of the Courses

Biology curricula in Egypt still emphasize a content of morphology and anatomy. An analysis of the content might suggest that there is much relevant to health, but it follows a strictly logical sequence with little application to real-life situations. The information within the logical structure is to be memorized as is other information in science. It is not included with the main purpose of improving the health of the learners.

To give an example to illustrate this, it is well-known that bilharzia is one of the most serious diseases in Egypt. The people who should be informed of its life cycle, its effects on human health, and the suffering and the lack of productivity which it causes are the youngsters at school age. Yet in biology teaching, bilharzia is merely presented as a "flat worm" in the sequence of invertebrate orders. Its relationship to human health is shyly presented as a secondary issue. If curriculum planners realize the gravity of such a parasite and how much damage it does to human health, and to the economy of Egypt, they should change the emphasis of presentation from "just another worm" to a menace that does so much damage and should be controlled through many channels, most effective of which is education.

Another example to illustrate the same point is teaching the system of the human body, which is done mainly in grades 7–9. The structure of the system is thoroughly presented with all anatomical details. But there is almost no reference to hygiene which is of such importance to the nation's health.

Although there are references in the syllabuses to care of the human body, to nutrition, to parasites and bacteria, and to pollution, these are considered secondary issues. No major health concepts are clearly defined or developed through the years of study. Furthermore memorization is still the cognitive level most stressed. Research done at the College of Education at the University of Manoura by the writer shows that examinations in biology for the secondary school certificate stress memorization since 80% of the questions do so. The research also shows that 70% of the memorized facts are forgotten during the first year afterwards.

The well-being of students does not have much consideration in biology courses. Young people need to know certain biological facts of life at certain ages in order to meet and solve the problem which will face them. Facts about reproduction, family life, growth, development, diseases and similar issues are hardly mentioned in biology courses. This causes considerable emotional problems for students, especially in the secondary school.

Community health is also an issue of only minor importance in the biology curricula. It is only a few years ago that pollution was first mentioned in 10th grade biology. Marriage, heredity, sanitation, family planning are not mentioned in biology courses.

Skills, Habits and Attitudes

Developing proper health skills, habits and attitudes is not one of the objectives of biology teaching in Egypt. Skills and attitudes related to nutrition, to sanitation and pollution control, to protection against contagious diseases, to child care are rarely mentioned. Since the teaching process is directed mainly towards passing the examinations, and since skills are not emphasized in examinations, it is understandable that teachers do not give them much attention.

Unfortunately students do not usually learn proper skills and habits from their families or their communities. This makes it vital to develop them through the school curricula. Egypt is not the only country in this respect: it is likely that, in all developing countries, schools should play a larger part in this. Biology educators should determine what are the basic skills and habits, and set them as important objectives to be achieved by the school. It should not be left to mere chance, or to the personal outlook of individual teachers to deal with matters so important to health.

Curriculum planners in Egypt hardly pay any attention to the development of attitudes. Research however at the University of Minofia has shown that biology teaching can develop such attitudes and an experiment in the schools of Minofia gave very encouraging results. It showed however that biology teachers must be trained for this both at pre-service and in-service levels.

Teachers, of course, are the important factor, especially as the teacher's role is not confined to the classroom. Their own attitudes and habits have a profound effect on students. Unfortunately they are not always a good example, drinking unsanitary water on field trips or eating unwashed fruit or vegetables.

Teachers can also promote respect and understanding of medical services in the community. The role of the biology teacher in giving guidance is too often absent. Students in most cases do not dare to ask their teachers about problems causing them anxieties in their lives. Questions about sex, family life, growth and development are among the important questions that the biology teacher should answer very frankly and scientifically.

Conclusion

An effective system of education should be able to change students' behaviour. It might be expected that a youngster who studied bilharzia at school would refrain from doing things which expose him to infection. This, unfortunately, is not always the case. Children in the villages study bilharzia at school and go the same day to swim in canals infested with the parasite. The percentage of infected students is as high as among other sectors of the population.

Biology education in Egypt is not contributing as much as it should to health. We need to re-think our courses. What health concepts should be in the curriculum? To give them proper emphasis they will need to replace some of the traditional logical structure of biology. Furthermore memorization should not be the focus of concern of teachers and students: higher cognitive levels should be sought. This may lead to changes of attitudes and hence changes of behaviour. Above all guidance must be given to teachers through pre-service and in-service training.

13

Environmental Aspects of Health Education

W. K. KING

University of the West Indies, Barbados

Human beings, by their activities, by their lifestyles and by their unending quest for "progress", have disrupted the stability that naturally exists between the environment and themselves. This disruption does not only harm the environment, but it precipitates a myriad of disorders in the human beings themselves. Present-day writings, both scientific and popular, are full of examples of such instances of disorder and instability: the pollution of the environment; poor sanitation; acid rain; an explosive population rise. All these are familiar.

The question arises: how do we redress the imbalance between mankind and the environment? Some people think that already it is too late. Probably a more realistic question is: how do we prevent further disruption and dislocation? A positive answer to that may be in education at all levels: education which transcends the narrow bounds of traditional schooling, but which changes behaviour patterns.

As emphasized elsewhere in this book, a healthy life is very dependent on a healthy environment, as it is on other factors. A positive attitude towards the environment is therefore an important component of health education. It is the author's view that health education is an aspect of a totality called "environmental health". The two should not exist in water-tight compartments. A symbiotic relationship between biology, health education and environmental education is vital for all three: biology informs the other two areas, itself drawing on examples and instances from them.

Health and Environmental Education in the Caribbean Region

Health and environmental education have in recent times been important talking points throughout the Caribbean region. Statements of intent have been made: yet, for all the pronouncements and promised activity, the status of these two areas has shown little change for the better. True, some countries have included aspects of "Health and Family Life" in their curriculum. Also true, there is a prevalent philosophy that certain subject areas should be taught with an environmental slant. However the amount of time given on the timetable and the overall inadequacy of teacher preparedness do very little to improve the position.

In certain Caribbean countries there is a movement towards integrating health education with established programmes in science, social studies and home economics. The reasons are mainly to economize on time and to give the programme some enhanced status. Table 1 shows the marked commonalities which exist in these areas in the curriculum at present. However the mere statement of topics does not mean that the essential aspects of health are being taught in the schools. There is a strong case for a new philosophy, incorporating health education, together with environmental topics, into the teaching of biology.

Schaefer (1980) in tracing the development of biology teaching has pinpointed certain well-defined movements. There were the interdisciplinary structures of the 60s, through the transdisciplinary thrust dictated by "problem fields arising from urgent needs of the individual or society", to the environmental education of the 70s. He identifies a third movement in the 80s, a movement towards new and effective forms of health education. Schaefer summarizes the new movement thus:

> "Of course there has always been health education in previous decades of biology instruction, in textbooks mostly at the end of chapters on specific organs . . . However, this kind of health education remained quite subject-specific, confined to the anatomy and physiology of malfunction. Thus biology teachers, according to their textbooks, treated questions concerning health from this viewpoint alone. They contributed to the understanding of bone fractures and distortions through the laws of levers, or to an understanding of smoking diseases through the pharmacology of nicotine . . . Only very few teachers, the real educators among the biologists, dared to proceed to the deeper causes of disease which mostly lie in the field of social psychology."

There is a strong case for delivering health and environmental education through science, and especially through biology, for two main reasons: first, the pressure on the school curriculum; secondly, because of the overlap in each of the areas.

One of the more recent attempts to bring these issues into school biology teaching has been the development of a syllabus for the Caribbean Examinations Council, which does suggest by implication a place for health and environmental topics. However close scrutiny of the specific objectives seems to indicate that the aspects of health and the environment are being treated for their biological content, rather than proceeding to the deeper causes of disease and environmental problems. The emphasis is on a study of major diseases, their causes and control. The concept of health seems focused on disease rather than on the positive sides of health education towards which much reference has already been made in this book.

TABLE 1 *Comparison of Topics on Health, Science, Social Studies and Home Economics in the Curricula of some Caribbean Teachers' Colleges*

Health and Family Life	Science	Social Studies	Home Economics
Human Growth and Development	*Form and Function*		*Child Growth and Development*
– Anatomy and physiology – Phases of development – Personal hygiene – Physical fitness – Genetics – Personal development	– Structure and function of circulatory, respiratory, excretory and reproductive systems		– Development of the foetus – Physical, social and mental development of the child – Protein – calorie nutrition – Childhood infections e.g. parasites, anaemia, immunity
	Growth and Development		
	– Asexual reproduction; binary fission – Balance and living things		
Food and Nutrition	*Modes of Nutrition*		*Food and Nutrition*
– Concept of food and nutrition – Food needs of the body – Functions of food – Classification of food – Local food production: supply and cost – Dietary needs and food selection – Digestion, assimilation – Food preparation, hygiene and storage – Nutritional problems – Food facts and fallacies	– Energy, food and fuel – Autotrophic nutrition – Heterotrophic nutrition – Holozoic nutrition – Saprophytic nutrition – How do parasites feed? – How do symbionts feed? – Symbiotic bacteria and fertility in soils		– The value of food – Classes of food – Digestion – Methods and effects of cooking – Calorific values of common foods – Recommended nutrients; balanced diets – Food storage; food preservation; kitchen hygiene – Major food groups – Infant nutrition – breast feeding – Weight control

Health and Family Life	Science	Social Studies	Home Economics
Environmental Health	*Social Implications of Science and Technology*	*Resources*	
– Water supply	– How much energy do we consume for domestic purposes?	– Culture	
– Food hygiene	– Water – a precious commodity	– Conservation	
– Waste disposal	– Pure vs impure water	– Pollution	
– Pollution	– Local drinking water	– Renewable resources	
– Housing	– The sea	– Non-renewable resources	
– Pest and vector control	– Soil conservation	– Production	
– School sanitation	– Use of fertilizers	– Exploitation	
– Health laws	– Social implications of forests	– Labour	
– Public amenities	– Conservation of wildlife	– Land, labour and capital	
– Drainage	– Alcohol and tobacco		
– Protection and conservation of environment	– Drugs: use and abuse	*Tourism*	
	– Smoking		
Human Relationships	– Ecological relationships	*Social Groups*	
	– Interdependence		
– Family		– Socialization	
– Human sexuality		– Social interaction	
– Interpersonal relationships		– Roles	
– Rights and responsibilities		– Norms	
– Problem-solving and decision-making		– Change	
		– Interdependence	
		– Groups	
		– The family – unions, divorce, family law, stratification, changes in family patterns – family planning	
		– Factors influencing family life	
		– Population problems related to adequate social services	

Mental Health and Drug Abuse

– Psychological development
  and its relation with somatic,
  environmental and social
  factors
– Life-coping skills and needs –
  defence mechanisms
– Roles and interdependent
  relationships of family
  member
– Mental illness, treatment and
  rehabilitation
– Myths about mental illness
– Use of substances that
  modify behaviour
– Legislation

Consumer Education

– Home management
– Services
– Advertising

Health and Social Services

– Health services
– Other social services/facilities

Drugs: Use and Abuse

– Alcohol and tobacco
– Smoking
– How does man affect the
  environment?

Home Management

– Money management
– Advantages of budgeting
– Consumer education related
  to shopping
– Food costing

Health and Family Life	Science	Social Studies	Home Economics
Population Education		*Population*	
– Size, composition and distribution		– Change	
– Vital statistics		– Migration	
– Levels of fertility		– Acculturation	
– Socio-economic interrelationships		– Conflict	
– Employment		– Urbanization	
– Legal aspects		– Demography – sources of data	
– West Indian family		– Population growth	
– Planning		– Population structure	
– Natural disaster		– Population control	
		– Population distribution	
		– Population movement	
		– Population problems related to food supply, adequate social services, labour supply	
		– Demographic theories	
		– Demographic patterns in the Caribbean	
Safety and First Aid			
– Safety in the home, school, etc.			
– First Aid			
Dental Health	*Dental Formulae and Denition*		
– Structure and formation			
– Growth and development			
– Oral care and hygiene			
– Dental disorders			
– Use of dental health services			
– Preventive measures			

Health Problems –
Recognition, Prevention and
Management

- Communicable diseases
- Non-communicable diseases
- Disabilities and defects
- Behaviour problems
- Prevention and management
  (Immunization, hygiene,
  etc.)

Diseases

- What are contagious and
  infectious diseases?
- What are the causative
  agents of disease?
- How are diseases spread?
- Prevention of diseases

Child Health

- Causes of childhood illness;
  hygiene, poverty, education,
  climate, customs, heredity,
  nutrition

Childhood Infections

- Causes and prevention of
  deficiency diseases

Various authors have suggested ways and means of bringing about the infusion of health education into biology teaching and one such scheme is given opposite. Table 2 suggests a scheme for bringing both health and environmental aspects into biology teaching.

The ideas outlined so far about bringing health and environmental issues into biology teaching seem fine in theory, but are they feasible in the real classroom situation? This brings us to the kernel of the problem. In the Caribbean there are tremendous barriers to implementation, including teacher training, societal attitude, apprehension of teachers to handling controversial issues, how to evaluate progress.

The treatment outlined requires new knowledge and skills in teachers and this means well planned and effective teacher training programmes, both in-service and pre-service. What is even more important is the need to change attitudes. Some of the topics proposed impinge on areas formerly reserved for social scientists. Some present biology teachers are very reluctant to handle such topics which are not entirely within their area of training. Changes in attitudes and values take a very long time.

In the classroom, evaluation is an important aspect of the whole teaching/learning process. Unfortunately too much of it measures merely the cognitive domain of learning, too little even attempts to measure the affective. This deficiency will be even more disastrous in health and environmental education. To evaluate a programme geared towards health and environmental education requires that one looks for indicators of healthy living and improved environmental awareness. Perhaps the best indicator of these is demonstrated by the type of lifestyle exhibited. There is a distinct difference between knowing that certain food substances are injurious to health and making a conscious effort to avoid these in your diet.

What is advocated here is a shift of biology from comparative studies to social biology and environmental sciences. It represents a shift away from "knowledge studies" to "issue studies". Such a shift from the pursuit of biology primarily for its own sake towards its implications and applications and the way it can undergird health and environmental problems requires a new set of skills and attitudes amongst teachers. The challenge is great, but inescapable. Social relevance must become the *raison d'être* of biology if it is to avoid losing its pivotal role in the education of citizens.

Reference

Schaefer G. (1980) "The Concepts of Health and Environment in Future Biology Teaching". Proceedings of the 8th Biennial Conference of AABE.

TABLE 2 *A Curriculum Scheme for Environmental Education through Biology Teaching*

Biological Topics	Suggested Environmental Topics	Suggested Activities	Skills and Attitudes

Ecological relationships
Biotic and abiotic factors
Population. Human population
Impact of human population
  growth on natural resources
Pollution of air, sea, beaches,
  swamps
Conservation
	Environment and Environmental
	* Conservation*
	The meaning of environment
	The meaning of conservation
	Natural resources – renewable and
	  non-renewable
	Natural resources – incl. examples
	Non-renewable resources
	Conservation of natural resources
	The environment and future
	  survival
		Field trips to areas of renewable
		  resources
		Use of resource personnel from
		  environmental agencies
		Film presentations on effects of
		  man's activities on the
		  environment
			Strategies for conserving natural
			  resources
			Appreciation that some resources
			  are non-renewable and must be
			  used wisely
			Awareness that all resources must
			  be conserved

What is soil?
Soil formation – weathering
Constituents of soil. Soil types
Loss of fertility. Conserving and
  renewing soil fertility
Soil conservation and methods
	Soil – Erosion and Conservation
	Formation, classification of rocks
	  and soils
	The soil as a natural resource
	Utilization and management of
	  soils
	Chemical, mechanical weathering
	Effects of soil erosion
	Conservation of soil
		Field trip to soil conservation
		  station
		Charts, posters, exhibits on soil
		  conservation
		Simulations of soil erosion using
		  uncovered slopes
		Display of various minerals and
		  rocks
			Appreciation of the need for
			  effective soil management and
			  conservation
			Appreciation of the role of
			  individual, communities and
			  international organizations in
			  soil conservation
			An awareness of the importance
			  of the soil

Cultivation of the soil for
  agriculture
Animal husbandry
Crop rotation
Multiple cropping – pros and cons
Garbage – disposal and its effect
  on the environment
	Land – Use and Misuse
	Land use and capability
	Effects of marginal land farming
	Indiscriminate dumping of waste
	  on land
	Multiple land use
	Resolving conflicts from
	  competing land use
		Visit to site of indiscriminate
		  dumping on land
		Debate on "Competition for land
		  use"
		Role-playing
			Awareness that the land is an
			  important resource
			Appreciation that misuse of land
			  may lead to problems

Biological Topics	Suggested Environmental Topics	Suggested Activities	Skills and Attitudes
Conservation of wildlife The useful aspects of wildlife and wild places Aesthetic appreciation of wildlife Protection of wildlife National Parks Preservation of habitat Reduction in the rate of loss of resources	*Wildlife – Destruction and Protection* Wildlife as a biotic resource Requirements for survival of wildlife Effects of human activity on wildlife Educational recreational and commercial value of wildlife Protection of wildlife – laws and statutes Wildlife which need protection in your country	Field trip to a disturbed area where wildlife is threatened Films etc. to reinforce the need for wildlife preservation Survey of the wildlife present in the country e.g., turtles, lobsters, sea-eggs	Development of a respect for wildlife, its conservation and management Appreciation of the educational, recreational and commercial value of wildlife
Effects of deforestation on the environment Tropical forests – conservation and management Plants as producers in the environment Uses of vegetation and forests Classification of Caribbean vegetation. Using simple keys	*Vegetation – Importance, Destruction and Conservation* Types of vegetation – natural and human-created Variation in natural vegetation in the Caribbean Classification of natural vegetation Detrimental effects of man's activities Importance of vegetation – watershed, soil protection, home for wildlife etc. Forests as gases maintainers in the atmosphere Consequences of destruction of vegetation Conservation of forests and other vegetation	Visit to land cleared for housing etc. Slide/tape development and presentation of effects of man's activities on vegetation Use of resource personnel to conduct field trip, and to suggest ways of conservation	Awareness of the need to judiciously manage the environment Ability to use keys to identify flora Willingness to tell others about consequences of indiscriminate destruction of forests and other vegetation
Water pollution – sewage, industrial wastes, metals,	*Water – Pollution and Management*	Research on how the country gets its water supply	Ability to determine pollution levels in streams, rivers, sea, air

Methods of preventing water pollution	Water as a habitat for plants and animals Pollution by domestic and industrial activities Conservation and preservation of freshwater resources	Visit to sewage disposal plant, irrigation station, factories (especially those that produce heavy smoke), marine ecological station e.g., Bellairs in Barbados	Awareness of the vital importance of water, air for survival
Air pollution. Main air pollutants – dust, smoke, sulphur dioxide, carbon monoxide, lead, cigarette smoke, radiation Reducing air pollution and its hazards	*Air – Pollution and Preventive Measures* Air is vital to all living organisms Harmful pollutants in the air Corrective and preventive measures for problems of air pollution	Use of resource personnel from bodies such as: Parks and Beaches Commission, Environmental Department, Conservation Department Slide/presentation on pollution – its effects and prevention	Awareness that man by his activities may leave a polluted earth for succeeding generation Understanding and appreciation of the effects of upsetting the balance in the ecosystem
Food from the sea. Fish farming. Major pollutants – sewage, oil, chemicals, industrial waste. The sea as an important ecosystem	*The Marine Ecosystem – Destruction and Preservation* Seas and Oceans – uses for man Seas and oceans as natural habitats Upsetting the natural balance in the sea		
Polluting effects of hurricanes –dust, sewage overflow, disease organisms Polluting effects of volcanoes – sulphur dioxide, volcanic dust, heat Fertility of volcanic soils Disaster preparedness and management	*Natural Disasters and their Effects on the Environment* Disastrous effects of hurricanes and volcanoes Volcanoes and soil fertility Restoration of disrupted environment – conservation and management	Simulation activities Pictures of the aftermath of hurricanes and volcanoes Use of resource personnel from Meteorological Department and Seismic Unit	Realization that pollution may be caused by natural sources, and occurrences
Conserving and preserving the earth and its resources Individual roles in conservation and preservation	*Looking Ahead* National and international environmental organizations – UNEP, CCA Finding urgent solutions to major global problems Preserving the earth and its resources	Debates, panel discussions, lectures/demonstrations involving, if possible, personnel from various national and international agencies	Appreciation that the earth's survival depends on global activities, but also individual ones

14

Re-defining the Boundaries of Health

M. N. BRUMBY
Monash University, Australia

If we want to educate the next generation to be able to examine critically and to resolve the problems created by the tidal wave of biotechnology, there are several preliminary steps. First we need to break down the taboo on death and dying. Death belongs to all stages of life. As Sir Macfarlane Burnet, one of Australia's greatest biological scientists said in 1978:

> "There is a nearly universal taboo against the discussion of death; . . . the time seems almost ready for that taboo to be lifted in the same way as the taboo against the public discussion of sexual matters has been over the past two decades."

The study of death is not yet part of school Biology, even though the legal definition of death is totally in terms of biological concepts.

Certainly it would seem desirable to counteract the image of death as violent destruction, which masquerades as news on nightly TV. Unless and until we take this step I do not believe we can begin to rationally discuss the sanctity- vs. quality-of-life debate, the distinction between compassionate killing and letting die, or the selective use of scarce, high-technology medical resources.

Associated with this, we need to include the normal human response to great personal loss, which is grief. (Over 10% of Australian couples have to learn to accept the lack of their presumed fertility. Furthermore, there are a tragically high number of school students who are learning to live through the loss of one of their most important possessions – a stable and loving home – through divorce. This surely must come into any definition of mental and social well-being.)

Secondly, we need to identify core concepts and principles which should be included within health education, particularly those that go beyond the physical dimension. A topic approach often omits the underlying concepts.

Thirdly, we need to consider re-defining the boundaries of health to include legal, social and ethical aspects of high-technology medical care which is part of the health care of the community. The term "human bioethics" has been coined to cover such studies of the impact of biotechnology on our society. It is an interdisciplinary approach. What are the implications for teachers if human bioethics were to be included in the curriculum?

The idea of interdisciplinary studies is not new. It means being able to raise controversial issues in the classroom, which for health teachers also is not new. It will mean further studies, for as it has been shown in the area of drug education, it is not enough to be armed only with "good intentions".

There are some encouraging signs. In the 1960s we became increasingly aware of the impact of technology on the natural environment. Out of this concern grew the conservation movement, which clearly valued our natural heritage. It took some 7–10 years after that for Environmental Science to be introduced. The curriculum is interdisciplinary, including biological and ecological concepts, geographic, economic and political aspects. It sets out an approach to environmental problems, analysing issues, evaluating alternatives before coming to decisions, which may have to be taken in spite of incomplete knowledge. Although at higher levels the subject Environmental Science has always been small, it has had considerable effect on junior secondary science in Australia. Scarcely a student leaves school today without having studied some aspect of the impact of technology on the natural environment.

Now in the 1980s we are becoming aware of these new issues. Again they are interdisciplinary. In addition to biological, scientific and medical aspects, they have social, legal and ethical implications. Will a place be found for them in the curriculum?

In conclusion, the great majority of our community, and of students leaving school are ignorant of human biology, of scientific developments which will re-shape their lives, and of the wider implications of such technologies. They are also leaving school ignorant of the law as it affects their health care, of their rights and responsibilities as citizens and future parents, and of the important values and philosophies on which society is based.

One of the issues in bioethics is whether it has a place in schools. I am convinced that it has. Unless and until we review our school curricula to include these areas, we are failing to educate the next generation, or even to prepare them for the world in which they will live. Our generation has barely begun to formulate the questions in order to see where we are going as we approach the year 2000, let alone to decide whether we as a community want to go in that direction.

The real challenge is not if, but how: how to encourage youthful minds to think creatively and critically about science and technology and their applications to human life.

15

The Career-Line in Health Education

T. WILLIAMS
Southampton University, UK

The many reports concerning health matters which have come from national and international organizations over the past years have repeatedly emphasized the important role of the school in alerting young people to their responsibilities for their own health care. Several points emerge from a reading of these documents which have an important bearing upon the perception of health education which teachers and schools might develop.

First, the changing pattern of illness and disease over the past three decades, which places a greater emphasis upon the need for individual responsibility for health-related behaviour. This has been characterized by a decline in relative importance of the infectious diseases and an increase in the behaviour-related diseases such as, for example, the use of tobacco and its association with lung cancer and bronchitis, emotional problems associated with poor personal relationships, accidents, alcohol-related problems, sexually-transmitted disease, heart disease and many others.

Secondly, many of these diseases can be associated with lifestyles adopted by individuals, groups or families. In the sense that these are associated with individual patterns of behaviour, they are largely preventable, in theory at least. Individuals and groups do have choices whether to smoke or not, whether to take exercise or not, and in many other ways whether to expose themselves to the risk of disease or illness. In this way health education may be interpreted broadly as effective training in decision-making.

It is also important to emphasize that some potential and some real health problems are created by societal and industrial factors over which the individual has little or no control. Food additives or the toxic products of industrial processes provide prime examples of potential hazards to health which are not amenable to individual decisions. There are larger societal and political issues which require corporate decisions: corporate decisions which nonetheless can be, and often are, influenced by determined individuals or groups working together in a joint purpose for the common good.

Thirdly, an inherent difficulty of many of our contemporary health issues is that they are rooted in the social and cultural life of society itself. Health education can, too easily, be seen as a means of social first aid in which we are content to deal with problems only after they have become manifest. The "career line" is a concept which may usefully be borrowed from the social sciences to help in identifying the social antecedents of some of the problems. Such a career line shows how patterns of behaviour can evolve through interaction with one's social environment. For example, the career line below shows the influences at various development stages which may affect, positively or negatively, the decision whether or not to use tobacco.

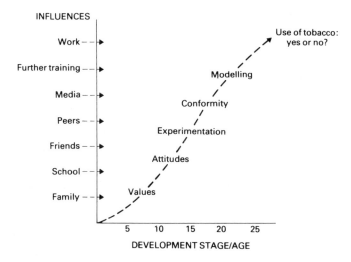

Generally the career line approach to health behaviour can be said to focus attention on the social, psychological and other factors which may influence the development of health-related behaviour. An excellent example of where this approach to health education would be of benefit is within the context of sex education. We have witnessed an almost interminable public debate in the UK for the past decade about whether or not sex education is appropriate for schools. Put in the context of the career line approach, we can readily see that all children are subjected to a host of influences which effectively give them a sex education of sorts. Evidence supports the belief that even very young children have developed ideas about sex, and such ideas will be expanded considerably as children interact and exchange ideas about sex with their peers and receive "informal" sex information through the media. It is clear that *all* children receive a sex education of sorts whether we approve of the fact or not; indeed it is difficult for anyone to live in a community without assimilating values, attitudes and knowledge concerning the accepted or even deviant patterns of behaviour prevalent in it.

The "career line" approach applies equally to our other problems associated with health behaviour and we need to start our debate on health education from a point which accepts that children are already receiving – by living in society – an education of sorts in health matters. We often ask ourselves, in all seriousness, at what stage children are ready for sex education or ready for education about smoking, drugs, alcohol, etc, forgetting as we do so that they have, as research demonstrates, been exposed to a multiplicity of experiences out of which they are already formulating attitudes, values and possible future modes of behaviour.

The question we should ask is not whether health education programmes should be included in schools, but instead what, when and how to give the most sensible, the most sensitive and the most relevant health education available. A society which ignores the importance of health education within the context of what its schools might offer places a very low premium upon the value of its own health, happiness and well-being.

Consideration of a "health career line" helps us to set a school health education curriculum alongside other important influences upon pupils. In doing this, we acknowledge the continuity of the lives which children experience day by day and we remind ourselves that the health education curriculum is but one small, but important part of that continuity.

We need to consider therefore the following points. First, whether or not schools can be health-promoting communities, which depends very significantly on the total influences of the whole school – its traditions, its values, the way in which the school is organized – and whether they are supportive of the health education which is taught as part of the overt curriculum. Secondly, the influence of the family upon the values and the attitudes of their sons and daughters, and the importance of linking family life with what schools are about. Thirdly, the relationship of the health education curriculum to the wider society – its values, norms, beliefs and practices.

Taking smoking as an example, let us examine the implications of these points for our school health education programmes. We can represent some of the influences known to be important as follows:

   (i) permissiveness towards smoking by parents and their own examples to their children;
  (ii) the smoking habits of older siblings;
 (iii) the desire to conform with peer behaviour and experimentation;
 (iv) the persuasiveness of the media;

   (v) the smoking behaviour of reference groups and role models (pop groups, etc);

   (vi) the smoking behaviour of work colleagues.

A school which is mindful of these influences might decide to implement a programme of health education by agreeing to provide:

   (a) a school policy related to smoking – for all members of the school community;

   (b) peer-led tutor groups;

   (c) positive teacher models (see (a) above);

   (d) school/parents initiatives – supported by the school health service;

   (e) in secondary schools, smoking cessation "clinics".

Further consistency between school and community might be achieved by community action concerning smoking in public places and some attention to the portrayal of smoking in the media. It is possible in these ways to acknowledge that schools cannot be totally effective on their own: there is need to consider how school health education can support what the community itself is committed to.

16

Can Western Medicine be made Compatible with Traditional Beliefs?

H. V. WYATT
University of Leeds, UK

The germ theory of disease is one of the pillars of western medicine. Although the theory as such is only 115 years old, the idea of infection and infectious disease is much older and was a strand in a tradition of medicine. This was partly because in temperate climates many infectious diseases were epidemic and recognized as such. In tropical and semitropical climates, however, many of the common infectious diseases are endemic and their infectious nature is masked.

Although western medicines such as injections and drugs have been enthusiastically absorbed in developing countries, the concepts of western medicine have not been accepted, but rather ignored.[1] Traditional medicine and beliefs grew out of a complex balance of environment and social structure. Western medicine cannot easily replace them without upsetting the balance of society, as shown by the population explosion and the growth of towns. If western medicines were neutral, their adoption might be expensive but not injurious. Unfortunately, many are toxic, others are selective of resistant organisms while injections may cause abscesses, provoke poliomyelitis[3] or produce septicaemia. The indiscriminate use of unsterile and dirty (if not filthy) syringes and needles is widespread by traditional healers, nurses and even doctors. From 1914 onwards, there were massive campaigns to cure yaws by giving injections of the drug Salvarsan. The results were described as magical in many publications: the horrible cutaneous sores of yaws were cured in one or two weeks. Whole populations in the yaws belt across the world began to clamour for injections. It is very probable that the high incidence of Hepatitis B virus in Central Africa is due to its transmission from person to person by dirty, contaminated syringes. The emergence and transmission of the deadly Ebola Virus and the AIDS virus (HTLV III) in Central

Africa probably has the same origin. The mixture of traditional healing and western syringes has been lethal.

Clinical microbiology is a powerful tool and provided that specimens are handled correctly and carefully, working in a hospital laboratory is probably less risky for a British doctor than a holiday in the Tropics. But the *potential* for spread of bacteria and viruses is enormous unless all precautions are observed: three epidemics of smallpox are known to have been caused by escape of virus from two laboratories in England. Epidemics of other diseases originating from tropical laboratories would not be traced against a background of endemic disease. Safety precautions are often ignored or not implemented through lack of money. Staff smoke, eat and drink at the bench on which are clinical specimens or cultures. Staff do not wear protective clothing because it is too hot. There are no washbasins, soap or towels. Cultures of virulent pathogens are kept in the refrigerator next to unprotected food.[2] Although laboratory staff may have immunity, they may be infected and pass on organisms or viruses to their children or others. Western-trained staff who hold higher certificates or degrees from America or Europe behave as though they do not believe in the germ theory of disease.

When we teach science in Europe and North America, we do it against a cultural background of the germ theory of disease, reinforced by advertisements about "killing all known germs". In developing countries, there may be beliefs about disease based on a totally different concept of Man and Nature, although customs may reflect a pragmatic approach. For instance, certain families add a particular clay to Nile water for drinking. This causes flocculation and reduces virus concentrations to perhaps less than 0.1% of the original. The nature of the clay and the amount to be added, is told by mother to daughter. That such families suffer less illness is known by other villagers.

How can the two cultures be merged to ensure that the best of each is retained and not, as I suspect at the present, the worst? It is ironic that the catastrophic epidemic of AIDS has come not from the laboratories of the molecular biologists as feared, but from the universal misuse of the simple hypodermic syringe!

References

1. Wyatt, H. V. (1984a) The popularity of injections in the Third World: origins and consequences for poliomyelitis. *Social Science and Medicine* **19**, 911–915.
2. Wyatt, H. V. (1984b) Come back Semmelweis. *Medical Laboratory World*, August: 51 and 53.
3. Wyatt, H. V. (1985) Provocation of poliomyelitis by multiple injections. *Transactions of the Royal Society of Tropical Medicine and Hygiene* **29**, 355–358.

17

The Importance of Cloning and Biotechnology in Combating Disease

G. STOLTMAN and E. J. WOOD

The cloning of cells, molecular cloning and the use of biotechnology are likely to have far-reaching implications on health and medicine in the future. In this contribution we explain some of this technology in relatively simple terms so that the teacher can understand these developments and introduce them into the classroom.

Recombinant DNA Technology and Genetic Engineering

"Genetic engineering" is a phrase frequently to be found in the newsmedia these days. Many people have the impression that it is likely to have a profound effect on our lives in the next few decades, but few have the technical knowledge to understand the techniques, the potential and the possible hazards.

Since the discovery of the structure of DNA in 1953 by Watson and Crick, techniques have been developed by means of which it is possible to isolate a single gene from one organism and to transplant it into another. In the last 5–10 years people have started to realize the potential benefits of this. One could imagine the benefits to agriculture if it were possible to take the genes for nitrogen fixation (which presently are found only in certain bacteria) and transplant them into the plants. In the field of health care, many individuals suffer from "genetic diseases" such as sickle cell anaemia. Imagine the benefits if we could replace the "faulty" genes with the "correct" genes. In fact neither of these possibilities has been realized – yet. However, the science of Genetic Engineering is only in its infancy and some practical successes have already been achieved.

In the early days many people, including both scientists and politicians, were worried about possible hazards. What if someone were to transfer a gene capable of causing disease in humans into a common bacterium that could escape into the environment? Such possibilities certainly exist and there was, in some countries, an embargo on experiments. However, our increased knowledge of gene expression suggests that many of the potential problems can be overcome by the use of bacterial strains with such specific nutritional requirements that they could never live "in the wild". However, each case has to be viewed on its merits and the risks assessed. The initial overreaction has now died down to a large extent. Obviously we should not be complacent, but nevertheless the existence of such potential hazards makes it all the more important for debate to take place and for informed non-scientists to participate in it.

Each species of animal, plant and micro-organism has different information stored in its DNA (coded as a sequence of nitrogenous bases) and produces a different set of proteins. This is why species differ. Even a small change in the DNA (e.g. altering one base) can lead to a different protein being produced. In sickle cell anaemia a single base change in the DNA results in the production of a haemoglobin that has a diminished ability to carry oxygen. We would like to cut this mutated gene out and replace it with a normal one. However, since every human has millions of genes it was not possible until recently to identify the very small part of it that coded for haemoglobin. However, genetic engineering technology is changing this.

Methods now exist by which DNA can be cut and rejoined and hence genes can be isolated, modified and transplanted. The "tools" of this technology are the same tools the cell uses, namely enzymes, now available in purified form. Examples are "restriction enzymes" which cut double-stranded DNA molecules at specific points, enabling genes to be cut out, and ligases which can be used to re-join DNA molecules. Hence a gene can be "taken" from one molecule of DNA and "transplanted" into another. Such DNA with new bits in it, is called "recombinant DNA". Most experiments at present are done with bacteria which naturally exchange bits of DNA ("plasmids") with one another. Any genes, including human ones, can be inserted into these plasmids and then, when a bacterial cell receives such a plasmid, it has the potential to "express" the human gene. This has already been done for insulin. Instead of extracting insulin from animal pancreas, bacteria which have been given the human insulin gene, produce human insulin.

How can we identify one gene (i.e. one section of DNA) amongst millions? Ways of doing this have been developed. They are based on either selecting, or producing a copy, of all or part of the gene in question. Because of the ability of the complementary strands of the DNA to "recognize" each other, a "copy gene", radioactively-labelled, can be used as a "probe" to identify a single gene. The process of recognition is called "hybridization", and by using this method it is possible to identify the region of the chromosome where a particular gene lies.

Monoclonal Antibodies

Antibodies are proteins produced by certain kinds of white blood cells (lymphocytes) in response to the invasion of the body by "foreign" proteins or complex polysaccharides. Such invaders are called *antigens* and may form part of a bacterial cell wall, a virus, or in some cases a cancer cell. Specific antibodies recognize and bind to antigen, marking it so that it can be destroyed by the phagocytes.

Upon initial contact with an antigen, the body's immune system is stimulated to produce a specific antibody. Any given individual will have been exposed to very many antigens during his or her lifetime, and his or her blood will therefore contain thousands of different antibodies.

Because of their ability to recognize antigens specifically, antibodies raised in animals are useful tools in science. However, because any experimental animal's blood already contains many different antibodies it is very difficult to produce an absolutely pure, specific antibody by immunization. Serum which contains more than one type of antibody is said to be *polyclonal* because its antibodies were produced by lymphocytes of many different types. Each type of lymphocyte has the potential to divide repeatedly to form a *clone* of identical cells, all producing exactly the same type of antibody. A *monoclonal* antibody is just such an antibody, but until recently it was not possible to prepare such material.

Within the last 10 years however it became possible to "manufacture" monoclonal antibodies in the laboratory. Two types of cell are needed, both usually obtained from mice. One is the antibody-producing lymphocyte, but such cells will not live in laboratory tissue-culture systems. The other cell type, a myeloma, is obtained from a tumour of the antibody-producing tissue and is "immortal" in the laboratory. If these two cell types are mixed together in the right conditions they fuse forming a so-called *hybridoma* cell. This new cell has the ability to produce antibody over an almost infinite period, having inherited the characteristics from its parent cells (a) of being able to form specific antibody, and (b) of immortality. It is then necessary to select the particular hybridoma cell producing the desired antibody from amongst many millions of cells.

Once this has been done, that hybridoma cell can be grown up ("cloned") to produce as many progeny as one wants. These daughter cells, produced by binary fission, all produce exactly the same type of antibody. The monoclonal antibodies can then be harvested from the nutrient fluid in which the cells are growing and used for many scientific and medical purposes.

Applications of These Technologies

Recombinant DNA technology has found very wide use in biochemistry and genetics in the study of gene structure and expression. These are fundamental to the understanding of the human body and of the disease process. A recent example of where such work is bearing fruit is in the study of the so-called *oncogenes* which may be involved in human cancers. Recent developments in technique have made it possible, easily and rapidly, to determine the sequence of bases in DNA, and hence to relate gene structure to protein structure directly.

(a) Diagnosis of Inherited Disease

There are a large number of genetic diseases called "inborn errors of metabolism". They arise when an individual receives from one or both parents a faulty gene: the patient then lacks the ability to perform some important biochemical function. In the disease *phenylketonuria* the individual lacks the enzyme to deal with the amino acid phenylalanine. Such diseases are present at birth, are incurable (at present) although often treatable. If the individual survives and produces children, there is a high chance of misgenes being passed on to the next generation.

Where parents are known to be carriers of a genetic defect, "genetic counselling" is frequently used to make them aware of the risks if they have children. One possible course of action, depending on the wishes of the parents and on their cultural and religious principles, is to abort a foetus carrying the defect. Obviously such a decision is not taken lightly and the earlier in the course of pregnancy it can take place the better. Parents often do not know they carry the defect and it is only when an affected child is born that the problem is revealed. Thereafter a medical geneticist can usually predict the chances of subsequent children being affected. It is desirable for the defect to be detected before the birth of the first child and for this to be done early in the pregnancy. This is possible for a number of inherited diseases using recombinant DNA technology, if a suitable probe is available. A bit of placenta is taken (a non-traumatic procedure) and the DNA extracted. If the gene in question has the correct sequence of bases then a restriction enzyme that will cut it into fragments of certain sizes is found. The fragments can be identified using the radioactive probe. If the gene is absent or does not have the correct sequence then it will not be cleaved, or will produce fragments of different sizes. Identification of the correct fragment establishes that the infant will have the disease and a decision on whether or not to abort can take place. Once the probe is available the tests are comparatively easy to perform and do not require especially expensive equipment or high technical skills.

Over 500 genetic diseases are known and it is estimated that about half a million afflicted children are born each year throughout the world. Many of these can now be diagnosed prenatally using recombinant DNA technology. It is also possible to determine the sex of the foetus by an examination of the chromosomes. This is of great medical importance since many genetic diseases are sex-linked.

(b) Production of Biological Compounds

There are many biological compounds which have great importance in treatment of disease. Insulin for the treatment of diabetes is one example, and the anti-viral material interferon is another. Some of these compounds can be synthesized chemically, others can be obtained from animal sources, and the remainder must come from human tissue. However there are ethical, economic and medical problems, associated with all of these. The new biotechnologies allow the production of many of these compounds in a purer form, in greater quantities at less cost than has been available previously.

(c) Production of New Vaccines

Vaccines are widely used to protect individuals and populations against disease. Upon immunization, a person's body responds to a harmless variant of a disease-causing agent (e.g. attenuated, living polio virus). The body does not recognize the harmless nature of the agent and mounts a vigorous immune response, which endows active protection against the normal, disease-causing organism.

The two major difficulties in producing a vaccine are (1) growing the microbe in the laboratory and (2) rendering it harmless while maintaining its ability to stimulate an immune response. The ideal vaccine is composed of just that part of the organism which stimulates the immune response, that is the antigenic part, excluding the toxic component.

Genetic engineering technology now provides the tools for the production of isolated, pure antigens in quantities sufficient to use as vaccines, as has already been done with Hepatitis B vaccine. Nonclonal antibodies, in addition to many other uses, allow the relatively easy identification and isolation of the relevant antigens.

These two technologies are brought together in the production of a malaria vaccine directed against the Plasmodium sporozoite.

(d) Future Prospects for Gene Therapy

As already mentioned above, there are hundreds of genetic diseases and it would be good to be able to cure these by administering in some way the correct gene to individuals with the disease. This is in the future. A couple of attempts have been made and they received wide publicity, but it must be said that they were premature and were unsuccessful. What is needed is much more investigation at the basic level in order to understand how the task might be accomplished.

Further Reading

Mayer, W. V. and McInerney, J. (1984) *Genetically-based Biologic Technologies*. Paris, Unesco.

Watson, Tooze, and Kurtz, (1983) *Recombinant DNA: A Short Course*. Scientific American Books/W. H. Freeman, New York.

Walker, and Gaastra (1983) *Techniques in Molecular Biology*. Croom-Helm, London.

Yoxen (1983) *The Gene Business*. Pan Books, London.

18

Improving Village Life

U. N. JAJOO

Sevagram, India

The problems of bringing medical care and health services to the rural villages of India were highlighted by the experiences of an Indian medical student. She was a student who believed that medical education should include practical experience as well as "the theoretical discussions and ideological debates of medical school". As she described it:

"We wanted to choose a village and adapt its medical facilities in order to improve the health and quality of life in the village. At first we chose Pujai, a village 15 km from the college. We cycled through many 'nallas', walked on slippery banks and through mud, but still Pujai was nowhere to be seen. When my sandals broke and others got thorns in their feet, a sensible thought struck us: 'go back'. But we could not as our trip had the sanctity of a mission. Finally we reached Pujai.

"It was a small village. We told them why we had come and how we had come. There was instantaneous rapport: 'Come again doctors. We need you. Look, you can have two rooms for the dispensary. Have some tea.' We asked: 'What happens to your sick in the rainy season when the village is unapproachable?'. 'We let them die' was the answer. We wondered how we could possibly explain that people were dying untreated 15 km from a medical college. It was like being in a hospital, reaching out your hand as far as you could, but finding it could not stretch far enough to ring the bell for help. Our desire to do something for Pujai was very strong. However after we discussed all the negative points (bad road, long distance away, etc), we realized we had to make a different choice if we were to have any chance of success. We chose Nagapur which was only 5 km away, but we wondered what would happen in Pujai. Was it a death sentence for people in the village?

"After three years of working in Nagapur, we learnt the following. (a) Our medical education in the hospital is inadequate to equip us with the skills required in a rural setting. (b) Socio-economic factors (poverty) and the political system are major obstacles in the development of appropriate medical care. We learn little about this in medical school. (c) Medical problems are not felt as a priority need in a community and therefore participation by the people is difficult to achieve. (d) Our health education work brought home to us, though painfully, that it is the 'educator' who is uneducated. We, the scientists, look from our ivory towers towards the people's problems and tend to ignore totally their social situation. Health education sermons therefore become completely irrelevant for the village people. We realized that if we, the educators, had to live in their social situation, we would tend to behave as they do. (e) In a poor socioeconomic setting, the idea of self-reliance in health care activities is very difficult. Even with contributions from outside, the typical rural village cannot fully support its health care and community health education needs."

In summary, we who are health professionals tend to come from

111

urbanized, educated, middle-class backgrounds. Our innate need of food and shelter is always met. Therefore we think of other priorities – education, sanitation, health, the quality of life. Poor village folk, caught up in survival problems of the present, cannot appreciate the long-term values of health care and health education.

19

Another Cautionary Tale

The following is quoted from the *Teacher's Guide* of the Science in Society project in the UK. It is part of a letter sent by Sister Gillian Rose from a dispensary in Khulna in Bangladesh. Its simple message contributes towards identifying some of the problems in developing countries.

"We are having a run of children with severe Vitamin A malnutrition, some with eyes destroyed beyond repair. It is sad . . . little children going blind amongst the vitamin-rich greenery of Bangladesh. How hard it is to teach the mothers. Their age-old village mindedness is like a brick wall, thick and impenetrable. One spends ages with the mother showing pictures, teaching and encouraging. A few days later she returns . . . 'What did you give this child for breakfast?' 'Barley (or sago)' . . . All these tinned things! The mother devotedly feeding her children on things she can ill afford because she thinks things in tins must be good . . . we feel like weeping. We had a seven-year-old yesterday who had had no vegetables at all except potatoes.

"Busy morning clinic this morning. Daily, new half-blind and anaemic and swollen scraps brought in by doting mothers who believe ardently in tonics and injections and potions and fakirs and bewitchery, but cannot seem to understand that a child needs a good wholesome diet. One well-to-do family with a wretched baby of a year old, pale and crying with pain . . . 'Oh, yes, his father buys him a bag of biscuits every other day, and sometimes even brings him a tin of Horlicks.' The amazement when Ruba suggests a good wholesome meal with eggs, lentils and vegetables . . . 'Oh, he doesn't eat anything like that'."

PART IV

Case Studies

Introduction

This section contains a number of papers, long and short, which it is hoped will prove to be a source of ideas: it contains the result of varied experience in different regions of the world.

It begins with a statement of the aims and objectives for a Health Studies course in Australia, a discussion on health education in European schools, and brief statements on health education in Hong Kong and Mauritius. Dr. Sapianchai's contribution describes the use of health education as a suitable course for non-science students in secondary schools in Thailand.

The experience of a community project in a fishing village in the Philippines is the basis for the next paper, followed by accounts of two very different community projects from India.

Dr. Thier describes the use that can be made of a study of advertisements in promoting health education, and this is followed by two accounts, one from India and one from Nepal, of the use of the CHILD-to-child material. A description of two projects from the Lawrence Hall of Science precedes a final description of a teaching unit on population from Israel.

EH-E

20

Health Studies in New South Wales, Australia

G. R. MEYER
Macquarie University, Australia

For some decades Health Studies have had a strong focus in programmes of the primary and secondary schools in New South Wales. At the primary level health has long featured as a major strand of the total curriculum. In the Junior Secondary School Years 7 to 10 it has had a well-organized separate identity linked closely to Physical Education as well as being taught through the agency of more established disciplines such as Science, Home Economics, Social Science, Language-arts and so on. In the Senior Secondary School Years 11 and 12 there has never been a separate discipline of "Health Studies" but a new programme is being devised for the Higher School Certificate. The main thrust has been through Physical Education and through contributions made by traditional disciplines, especially Biology, Home Economics and the Social Sciences.

The aims and objectives of "Health Studies" are defined in the New South Wales Curriculum Statement as follows:

(1) The aim of *Health Studies*, pursued by the school, in partnership with the home and community is:

To guide the development of individuals in the context of society, towards a healthy lifestyle.

A *healthy lifestyle* requires more than the acquisition of knowledge, concepts and skills. It encompasses the development of individual attitudes, values and effective social relationships.

(2) The objectives of *Health Studies* will develop in students:

- a range of physical skills which will increase body awareness and enable them to participate in a wide variety of activities of an aesthetic, recreational and sporting nature;
- a decision-making skill which will assist the individual to deal effectively with everyday life situations and contemporary health problems;
- competencies to adapt to change and cope with stress;
- positive attitudes and behaviour patterns regarding fitness and choice of recreational interests;

120   G. R. MEYER

> - a sense of personal and social well-being;
> - a responsibility for personal and social behaviour;
> - the ability to relate effectively with others;
> - expression and creativity through movement;
> - an awareness, understanding and acceptance of people with physical and mental disabilities;
> - positive relationships;
> - an appreciation of human performance;
> - an understanding and acceptance of individual differences;
> - individual responsibility for safety;
> - sport ethics including co-operation, tolerance and fair play;
> - effective communication through physical and social activities;
> - the ability to function confidently and effectively as a responsible community member;
> - understanding and development of a personal value.
>
> (3) In summary, *Health Studies* provides the individual with a basis for developing a satisfying healthy lifestyle which includes:
> - SELF ESTEEM
> - THE ABILITY TO MAKE WISE DECISIONS
> - PERSONAL FITNESS AND MOVEMENT SKILLS

A major recommendation of the draft Health Studies curriculum for New South Wales is that while the defined elements of the Health Studies programme should, themselves, be well integrated, they should be also reinforced and integrated where possible within teaching subjects across the curriculum.

It is this latter point which brings the Biology programme to centre-stage.

Secondary School Biology in New South Wales

In School Years 7–10, Biology is taught as a closely interwoven thread within a programme of General Science taken by all pupils. In Years 11 and 12 it is a popular optional subject in its own right and the majority of pupils elect it as one subject required for the Higher School Certificate. It can be studied as the only science or with Physics and Chemistry in a "double unit" multi-strand science course or with Physics or Chemistry as an alternative double subject. Whatever the form, Biology is popular, generally well taught and backed by excellent learning resources. It is equally popular with boys and girls and caters for a wide range of abilities.

During the seventies statements about integration with Health Education were less clearly defined by the Health Educators themselves. Biology programmes, however, were always cognizant of this responsibility. For example a typical statement of aims for Biology in School Years 11 and 12 included the following:

> 1.13 Knowledge of the impact of science on man and his culture
>
> . . .
>
> 1:133 Science is involved in the problems of man's survival
> 1.1331 disease and old age
> 1.1332 over-population
> 1.1333 racial problems
> 1.1334 misuse of resources
> 1.1335 supply of resources

And elsewhere in the same document,

> To maintain and develop interest in science and to develop scientific attitudes
> 2.1 Interest in science. Development of interest in
> 2.11 the methods of scientists
> 2.12 the content of science
> 2.13 the application of science to:
> 2.131 personal problems
> 2.132 community problems
> 2.133 national problems
> 2.134 international problems

These types of statements have continued into current syllabuses.

While very broadly defined these statements of aims do provide a clear opportunity for Biology programmes to stress aspects of health education. When taken together with statements in the parallel curriculum of Health Studies *per se* they not only provide an opportunity but a mandate and that, in fact, is how they have been interpreted. Clearly the two sets of aims are fully complementary.

Teachers in most schools in writing Biology programmes refer to health issues wherever possible consistent with both the Biology and Health Studies programmes. Textbook writers take the same view and most Biology books used in Australian schools give a strong emphasis to health aspects, frequently defined very broadly and fitting into a multi-level philosophy from individual to school and family, to local community to nation and to the international community. The public examiners for Higher School Certificate Examinations also give considerable emphasis to health aspects. The content of Biology has been used as a vehicle for achieving more significant aims such as developing problem-solving skills in socially meaningful areas such as personal and community development. This approach was especially the rule during the seventies when public examinations were seen in part as devices for speeding up the evolution of Biology teaching away from inquiry learning for its own sake towards inquiry learning for the achievement of meaningful socially relevant objectives.

21

Health Education in European Schools

T. WILLIAMS
Southampton University, UK

In attempting to review the "state of the art" in a European context it is evident at once that the development of school health education is uneven and patchy. At one end of the spectrum of development lies the implementation of school health education through national policy and legislation while at the other end some countries are still struggling to get health education accepted as part of school-based activities. Most countries are somewhere in between these two end points of the spectrum, grappling with its content and methodologies, trying to work out how to train teachers and others concerned and, not least, trying to convince schools and teachers of the importance of the introduction of health education into an already overcrowded curriculum.

There is a widespread agreement amongst all European countries concerning the need for national and local policies related to school health education. There is also total agreement concerning the need for a closer collaboration between the "education" and "health" authorities in each country related to such policies. While the responsibility for school health education nearly always lies with the education authorities, it is not unusual for the initiatives for such developments to come from the health authorities. These initiatives are often linked to community health issues, such as the use and abuse of drugs, alcohol and tobacco, for example. Indeed most European governments are highly motivated by the rapid increase in drug abuse and misuse and are eager for schools to take part in preventive action.

In some countries, such as France, Italy, Holland, England, Scotland, Germany and Ireland, independent organizations have been founded whose main purpose is to promote health education in the community. Often these organizations are funded from governmental sources and represent a commitment to the promotion of health which of itself can be seen as a broadly based policy. These centres for health education provide an excellent springboard for the development of school health education and ought to help solve the anomalies which still linger in the relationships between "education" and "health". There is considerable interest, therefore, in the legislation and consequent developments which have recently occurred in the Netherlands where health education shortly becomes an obligatory part of the primary school curriculum.

Policies are important in every country but have a special and particular part to play in countries where school health education is just beginning to develop. In some Mediterranean countries, for example, policies which link the system of primary health care in the community with health education and promotion in the school system are of particular benefit because they utilize the expertise and resources that are available in the most efficient and effective manner.

It is possible, then, to detect a cautious mood of optimism and a rising tide of interest in the promotion of school health education amongst both education and health camps. Indications of this renewed interest are *first*, the national discussions and pilot schemes which are now under way in every country and, *secondly*, the international activities which are sponsored by organizations such as WHO European Region, the European Economic Community and the Council of Europe. In the last analysis, however, it is for each country to determine its own policies and course of action within, perhaps, a framework of inter-European discussions and exchanges.

It is now generally acknowledged that the development of school health programmes rests upon the twin pillars of policy and training.

The lowly state and status of health education in European schools can be directly related to the paucity of training at both pre-service and in-service levels for all the professional groups concerned. While there are several interesting and exciting training activities going on in several countries, such as in England and Wales and the Netherlands, there is nevertheless need in all countries for massive and well-planned initiatives to redress what is generally agreed to be a poor situation. There is need for both pre-service and in-service training, but the latter is even more urgent because this provides the only means of improving the situation in schools in the short term.

The School as a Health-promoting Institution

The notion that one of the principal aims of the school should be to promote the health of its pupils is appealing in its simplicity. Few responsible educators would deny that schools have an important part to play in the promotion of the health of children. The reality of practice, in Europe generally, however, is that schools place great emphasis upon the academic and intellectual development of their pupils to the exclusion generally of matters related to their health and well-being. This is not to deny the progress which is gradually being made in the development, across Europe, of programmes of health education. These programmes are likely to be much less effective, however, if practised in schools whose structure, organization and values do not support classroom health teaching. It is clear that the major emphasis within Europe is still placed upon the development of a health education curriculum with its attendant materials and methods. More emphasis needs to be placed upon a consideration of the ways in which what is taught in the classroom might be supported and reinforced through the values and attitudes implicit in the organization, structure and staffing of schools.

In seeing the school as a community with some potential for promoting the health of children, it would be important to consider at least three ways in which it might be involved.

1. *The taught curriculum*   Clearly there is considerable scope for children and young people to acquire knowledge concerning how they might develop healthy lifestyles. Within this it would also be important to consider the place of values and attitudes and the methods by which teachers can best provide learning experience for their pupils.

2. *The other or hidden curriculum*   There are important ways in which pupils are influenced by the implicit values that are transmitted. For example, whether teachers show respect for each other and for their pupils; whether teachers practise what they preach; whether the school by virtue of its policies and practices places value upon the "health matters" it includes in its taught curriculum.

3. *Beyond the school gates*   No school can regard itself as an island immune to the behaviours and practices of the outside world. Families are important, communities are important and friends are important in helping young people to shape their ideas of what it is to be healthy.

The school wishing to see itself as a health-promoting community will need to consider carefully how, through its organization, management and policies, it can provide an environment conducive to the well-being of its pupils and staff. One important issue, for example, is related to the congruence between the aims of the school and those of the health education programme. Clearly these matters need airing by the teaching staff as a whole in order to allow discussion, debate and decisions to be made.

School as a Health-promoting Community

Aims for the School itself	*Aims for School Health Education*
To provide a healthful environment with regard to, for example, safety, meals, hygiene, buildings and grounds;	To promote a sense of responsibility in respect of the individual's, the family's and the community's health;

to provide exercise and leisure facilities;

to provide a positive social environment;

to support the health education curriculum;

to support the school health service and to develop its relevance to the health education of pupils.

to encourage a healthy way of life and present a realistic range of health choices;

to enable the learner to fulfil his/her physical, psychological and social potential and to improve self-knowledge and self-esteem;

to provide and develop capacities and skills, e.g. to make choices and decisions; to manage stress; to handle "conflictual" situations related to health;

to provide a health knowledge base, and skills in handling (i.e. obtaining, interpreting, using) information related to health.

School, Family and the Community

All European countries are crucially aware of the importance of setting school health education into the context of family life and the wider community. If this is not taken into account then health education which remains school-focused will be in danger of becoming sterile and irrelevant to the lives which children live outside school. This school–community interface does provide a formidable challenge for several reasons:

(a) because of the apparent discrepancies which exist between the health messages coming from a school health education programme and those coming through the media and, more clearly, perhaps, from the behaviour visible in the community and amongst families themselves;

(b) the difficulty experienced in attempting to involve parents with school initiatives in health education: rarely do the parents whom the schools wish to involve become involved;

(c) the reluctance of teachers to become involved with community dimensions of health education which might expose their limited competence and confidence in this area.

There is some support for the notion of linking school-based health education/promotion more closely with primary health care. This ought to be possible and desirable within all countries but might be particularly relevant in countries which have not yet fully developed their education or health care systems, or in which the health care facility might be supported by extra-curricular activities in countries with a particularly academically orientated education system.

There are several projects currently being developed which are attempting to bridge the school–community gap, for example, in Belgium in the context of nutrition education, another in England which seeks to involve parents in a dialogue concerning the content of what school health education is appropriate for their children, and in Norway where parents are actively involved in education about smoking.

Curriculum Development – Materials and Methods

Most countries are involved in some kind of curriculum development in health education involving the production of materials for schools. It is generally agreed that primary schools, because of their child centred approaches, are more receptive to health education than are the secondary schools. The organization and structure of primary schools are also more conducive to the development of health education, largely because of the stable relationships which are usually built between the class teacher and her pupils, and which provide a good platform for health-related work. Health education can be easily integrated with other areas of the curriculum because of the more flexible nature of the curriculum itself. Primary school science, for example, lends itself very well to an explanation of human biology and to the need for healthy lifestyles, as indeed do projects related to the environment. Perhaps the two areas of the primary school relatively unexplored in the context of health education are those of "language development" and "play". Both have tremendous potential as a medium for health education, particularly in the early years of schooling, and pilot work has already been established in England.

Secondary schools in contrast are constricted by the demands of *examinations* and often by a lack of strong teacher–pupil relationship bonds. The more able pupils receive a curriculum biased towards the traditional subject areas and which includes few, if any, activites related to their personal and social development. A consequence of this is that health education, if present at all, is more likely to be included in the curriculum of the less able pupils. This in turn results in health education becoming a "low status" activity – a perspective which must be changed if it is to secure a permanent and valued niche in schools.

An important point to emerge from European countries is that most do not view health education in schools as a separate subject. Indeed it is generally regarded as needing to be integrated with other curriculum subject areas. There are advantages to be gained from this in that there is less need for a timetabled slot in the school curriculum, but equally teachers will need to be convinced that health education forms a legitimate part of their subject teaching. In most instances it is possible to demonstrate that health education can provide an interesting dimension to other subjects and can usually enhance their relevance to the lives of the pupils.

There is much needing to be done in terms of developing health education in the context of the traditional subject areas. While some advances have been made in, for example, the biological sciences by the European Community's Biological Association, there is as yet an area of development relatively untapped by health education.

Even when health education is included in the curriculum, however, there remains the need for some kind of co-ordination in order to utilize what is available in the most efficient and effective manner – a task needing skills of diplomacy as well as those of curriculum development.

Developments in and across the curriculum, however, need to be matched by a consideration of the methods used to teach health education. Generally, it is now acknowledged that the didactic approaches, involving the learning of facts and figures, are alone not appropriate to health education. Health education is intended to help pupils assume more responsibility for their own lifestyles and, while appropriate facts are an important ingredient in the choices and decisions they make, this is only one part of the process. There is a considerable need for teachers and others involved in school health education to become familiar with and practised in methods more appropriate to health education – such as informal group work, discussion, simulation, role-play and decision-making processes and situations. It is clear that the production of suitable materials alone will not provide the evolution necessary in teaching/learning methods. There is need for basic training in the variety of methods available and necessary for the successful implementation of health education in schools.

In Europe then there remains much to be done but it can be seen that momentum is slowly building and real progress made through the exchange of ideas and joint developments.

The above is based, with permission, on a monograph compiled by D. T. Williams and C. de Panafieu on experiences in fifteen European countries and written for the WHO Regional Office in Copenhagen. It is published by the Health Education Unit, Southampton University, UK.

22

Health Education in Schools in Hong Kong

K. C. PANG
University of Hong Kong

In Hong Kong pupils go through 6 years of primary education, and health education is offered as a subject throughout those years. The curriculum is a well co-ordinated one with the following aims:

(a) to provide a basic knowledge of the organization of the human body and the requirements for keeping the body systems in a state of equilibrium;

(b) to develop good habits for maintaining physical health;

(c) to provide an understanding of common diseases and the methods for prevention and cure;

(d) to develop concrete attitudes and habits for mental and social health.

The topics of the curriculum revolve round major themes. In each year, pupils have a few topics under each theme, so that by the end of the 6 years they have acquired a comprehensive knowledge of each. The ten themes are:

Organization of the human body,
Personal hygiene,
Exercise and rest,
Growth,
Mental health,
Care of teeth,
Food and nutrition,
Safety at home and in school,
Prevention and cure of diseases,
Social hygiene.

An activity approach is used in teaching the subject and the teaching is pragmatic. Teachers place heavy emphasis on the pupils keeping themselves in good health, and a variety of programmes, apart from the teaching, is usually organized in the school to encourage good health in the pupils: election of "good" students; checking of cleanliness of nails, hair, uniform, etc by the teacher; awards for high standards and so on. The guidance officer in primary schools also organizes talks on various aspects of health. These measures, both formal and informal, provide a well-balanced initial health education.

Unfortunately, this is not followed up in secondary and post-secondary education. There is only informal health education in the secondary school. Some aspects of health are met in the biology syllabus, but those aspects are usually restricted to topics like micro-organisms and their contribution to disease. There are no specific objectives with regard to health education at these levels.

23

Health Education in Schools in Mauritius

M. ATCHIA
Mauritius Institute of Education

In Mauritius a new primary science curriculum was designed in 1982 to respond to current needs. Four main themes are used in it:

Basic science,
Health and hygiene,
Home economics and family life,
Agriculture and food.

The curriculum is now being developed: all lessons are integrated, that is they cover all the themes, including environmental aspects, and in many cases the social and historical aspects as well. For example, the lesson on personal cleanliness – the need to wash hands before meals and to bathe daily – is linked to water-filtration, chlorination and distribution (science), to the cost of tap water and the need to combat wastage (home economics) and to the importance of water in agriculture.

24

Health Education for Non-Science Students in Upper Secondary Schools in Thailand

N. SAPIANCHAI
Bangkok, Thailand

Background and Rationale

In Thailand, the upper secondary school students (Grade X–XII) have two main options, either to seek an academically oriented education or a vocationally oriented one. Among those who seek an academically oriented one are groups of students called non-science students; they are not interested in taking any of the regular science courses whatsoever. Yet, to prepare them for life, they still need a certain basic level of understanding and functional capability in science and technology. An effort had to be made to motivate them and to promote general scientific literacy. One way to begin, however, is to devise a science curriculum which has its style and content meaningful and relevant to the students' lives and interests. Realizing this, the Institute for the Promotion of Teaching Science and Technology (IPST) has developed the "Physical and Biological" science curriculum and offered it as an alternative to the discipline science courses.

The course materials are in modular form and include three modules concerning aspects of health, namely "Good living", "Medicine and life" and "You and your body". They are written to meet the needs and interests of adolescents. They need to value their bodies and to learn the basic principles of good health and disease prevention. They are interested in a healthy, attractive appearance which will affect their immediate personal lives and they are likely to form good habits if they have the necessary knowledge. A person with poor health will find less joy and less accomplishment in life and could raise problems for society. A nation,

133

especially a developing one like Thailand, needs manpower with fitness, mental poise and a wholesome social life.

With a positive approach to a healthy life, each of the three modules attempts to help students establish for themselves such attitudes, understandings and applications as the following:

(1) a sensible, objective attitude towards health, and a realization that a healthy body is worth much more than fame or money;

(2) an understanding of bodily structures, functions and needs;

(3) an appreciation of the importance of safety practices in day-to-day living;

(4) an awareness of the importance of nutrition, sanitation, personal hygiene and disease prevention;

(5) good habits to promote good health and overall personality;

(6) an understanding of narcotics and drug abuse, as well as general uses of medicine;

(7) a variety of cognitive, affective and psychomotor skills plus positive attitudes towards science.

The contents of the modules are as follows:
Good living:

Nutrients required by the human body. Carbohydrates; sugar, starch and cellulose; role of carbohydrate in the body. Fat; fatty acid; role of fat in the body. Protein; role of protein in the body. Vitamins, mineral salts and water. Proportion of nutrients required by the body. Food change; food preservation; food additives; poisonous substances.

You and your body:
The human machine. The body and its operation. Level of organization. The body systems. The integumentary system; skin structures, skin functions and skin care. The skeletal system; bones, joints and ligaments; bone care and promotion of good posture. The muscular system; function of skeletal muscles, muscular strength and muscular fatigue. The nervous system; the brain and spinal cord. Body energy.

Medicine and life:
"Good health is wealth". Longevity. Illness and the causes; illness caused by malfunctioning of the body cells; diseases caused by pathogenic micro-organisms. The body's defence mechanism. Vaccination and immunization. Medicine – the healing agents. Rules on medication. Herbal remedies – the natural medicines. Antibiotics – medicines derived from micro-organisms. Medicine obtained synthetically from chemical substances – antipyretics, antacids, antiseptics, disinfectants and common household medicines. Narcotic drugs, analgesics and drugs for an emotionally disturbed patient. The use of toxic

substances in exterminating disease carriers; plants' enemies and their environmental impact. Advances in diagnostic and therapeutic techniques – radiotherapy, radiodiagnosis, the use of lasers in surgery, the use of kidney machines in blood detoxification. Human spare parts for lengthening of life.

Each unit is planned to allow links between knowledge areas and daily experience of life. They use an inquiry and laboratory-investigative approach in order to make the students aware of the way scientists work. The laboratory investigations are usually carried out in groups of three or four. There are teachers' guides complementing each student book and these suggest outlines for pre-lab and post-lab discussions. They give additional background information for the teacher and details of advance preparation necessary for each activity. They also show how the major concepts in the course may be linked together.

Other suggestions are also made: about showing films or video tapes concerning certain aspects in order to stimulate class discussion; about getting pamphlets from local health agencies for class use or for the library; about inviting doctors to talk to the class; about encouraging students to organize a bulletin board of current magazine articles dealing with problems related to health; about inviting a dietician to talk to the class, followed by a visit to the school kitchen to see the methods of cooking to preserve vitamin content of foods; about getting students to make health check lists for their personal use; about getting posters designed to encourage good posture and to explain the harmful effects of bad posture.

The nationwide implementation of the course began in 1976. Follow-up and revision goes on continuously in order to make the textbooks more interesting and more appropriate to the students' needs. In general, students enjoy and accept the course as offered.

25

Environmental Aspects of Health Education in a Fishing Village

D. F. HERNANDEZ
University of the Philippines

The first part of this contribution describes the various aspects of a community project conducted in a fishing village. The second part deals with a study on the concept of health and environment of elementary students aged 9–11 and 12–14 in this village, and the implications such a study may have on teaching.

The Several Dimensions of a Community Project

The project described here took place over a 5-year period in a Philippine fishing village of 272 families, 85% of whom depended on fishing for their livelihood. It has only one elementary school and no high school.

The major objectives of the project were (a) linking school and community life by raising the level of scientific consciousness of the community and enriching the learning in school, family and community through meaningful activities; (b) general improvement of the quality of life of the people; (c) improving livelihoods; (d) community development. The project elements were:

1. A survey of the village, focusing on: occupations of the villagers; their beliefs and practices related to health, nutrition and occupations; community resources related to health, nutrition, sanitation, leisure-time activities, cultural and educational facilities; natural resources; skills and areas of competence the villagers wished to acquire in order to improve the quality of their life.

2. Analyses and planning based on the needs identified in the survey. The strategies included matching needs to resources available.

3. The project itself, which had various components. First, vocational and economic components related to fishing. Secondly, community health education components including seminars on diseases, maternal and child care, preparation of nutritious foods, organizing a medicinal plants garden, constructing water-sealed toilets, sanitation and garbage disposal, organizing a day-care centre. Thirdly, cultural and leisure-time components, including sports activities, library development, reading centres. Fourthly, educational components, including preparation and distribution of self-learning modules, organization of health and environmental activities, improvising science apparatus, for example desalination stills as an alternative method for securing pure water when needed. The final component involved evaluation.

Obviously an extensive project like this, involving many people with different interests, needs various types of personnel and strong links among the institutions and agencies involved. These were established at the national, regional and local level. The school principal was the major link to the school children and their teachers, and to the local community officials.

A significant element of this project was the involvement of the adults of the community throughout the project. They perceived the problems of the community in an adult way and they benefited from the project (economically and in other ways). The skills learnt were self-propelling: once learnt they could be carried on by the villagers themselves. They did not have to rely on external resources except in the initial stages and they were able to utilize materials and labour available in the community or nearby towns. The whole project encouraged the development of self-reliance.

The educational outputs of this project were considerable. Thirteen science education modules relating to community concerns were developed and used; twenty health modules were used and tested; the ones most crucial to the community were translated into the local dialect for use of adults in the reading centres in the community. The staff of the Department of Health were able to use the modules in other communities.

A Study of the Schoolchildren's Health and Environment Associations

A study was conducted in this community on the associations of health and the environment which the pupils possess. Since a major objective of the project was the linking of the learning which takes place in the school with the life of the community, it was considered important to conduct a study which would provide information on the interface between learning in the classroom with life in the community. It was felt that one way of securing information on this was through the free association technique, which has already been referred to in this book in Chapter 5. Any classroom teacher can use free associations very simply and it provides a means of finding out what goes on in the mind of the learners about what they are learning and the many associations these things have with the natural, socio-cultural and affective dimensions of their environment.

The total population of schoolchildren in two age groups present in school on the day of testing was used in the study. This included 77 pupils in the 9–11 age group and 44 in the 12–14 age group. The pupils were divided into three language groups: A – local language, B – national language, C – English language. Some of the interesting results are listed below.

1. Girls in the age group 9–11 gave more responses in the economic and socio-cultural dimensions than did the boys. The girls' responses included more responses with value-orientated associations, such as feelings of happiness, well-being, etc.

2. There were few imaginative responses in both age groups. Most responses were concrete objects or behaviours. Economic activities were specifically related to those available in the community.

3. Both groups associated desirable personal and social qualities like industry, courtesy, generosity, kindness, trustworthiness, helpfulness and other positive qualities with good health. A few negative qualities were included but these were minimal.

4. The majority of associations made by the pupils in regard to health, as well as the environment, relate to the various aspects of the project which had been in operation for over 2 years at the time the association test was administered; more were community specific and would very likely have been discussed in the classroom.

5. The English language group did significantly better than the two other language groups in the "Preventive measures" category in the health association section and the "Health-making environment" category in the environment associations. The local and national language groups gave more associations in the psychological, aesthetic, economic and socio-cultural dimensions. The influence of language on learning seems apparent here. Science and mathematics are taught in English, the other subjects in the national language. The associations of the English group seem to point to learning in the classroom, whereas the other two language groups had more associations in the psychological, aesthetic and socio-cultural dimensions which are likely not to be touched upon in science classes for these age groups.

A year later when the same test was administered to the same age groups, it was the category "Health-making environment" which drew a significantly higher percentage of responses (relative to environment associations).

Implications for Teaching

Using simple association techniques, the teacher can identify the associations students have of a given concept. This could be used as a base to start instruction. Students can be made aware that concepts can be viewed from a variety of viewpoints depending on the peculiar set of associations or relationships perceived by individuals, and this is affected by the nature and variety of their experiences. They can then be made to realize that a concept may have many meanings, and that in a given field of specialization some terms have special meanings accepted generally all over the world. But other meanings/associations (including those of the affective domain) are idiosyncratic, or have cultural meanings. The teacher can thus help students broaden their views of the world, beginning with the meanings they already possess (in the local or national language), by accepting these concepts as part of day-to-day life. Students will come to realize that there are cultural meanings, there are idiosyncratic meanings, and there are the specialized meanings of a concept peculiar to a discipline like science. These are the international or public meanings of concepts.

The ability to associate a variety of experiences with a given concept is to be encouraged. It could be a way to enhance lateral or divergent thinking in the students. It may also be that the richer the environment (in terms of opportunities for varied experiences), the more likely the student will have more associations and enriched meanings of a concept. This factor of an enriched environment is to some extent under the control of the teacher. It is, for example, enhanced by the variety of methods used, the learning materials (print and non-print) the teacher selects, and the general climate for learning provided in the classroom.

The result that showed more associations relating to health and the environment in the English language group, and more associations relating to the cultural, psychological, affective and social dimensions in the local and national language groups, could call attention to two modes or styles of learning. In the context of the community studied (as well as in the rest of the Philippines) English is used to teach science and mathematics; all other subjects are taught in the national language. Ramirez and Castañeda, have identified two cognitive styles which they have explained within the framework of field sensitivity and field independence. Field-independent behaviours and teaching styles are more appropriate to the teaching–learning of the sciences and mathematics whereas field-sensitive behaviours and teaching styles are more appropriate to the social sciences and experiences which can be humanized and personalized. To encourage field independence, for example, the teacher should use teaching styles that promote this quality such as: formal relationships with students, focusing on instructional objectives and encouraging independent effort. To develop field sensitivity, teaching styles which are personalized, which express warmth and approval, which encourage modelling and invitation could be used. The teacher should select subject areas or topics that lend themselves to these teaching styles with as much ease as possible.

Evaluation

In addition to the periodic evaluations already made on the project, an overall evaluation was made which involved representatives of all those involved in various aspects of the project. The highlights of the various reports were as follows.

On the positive side these were cited: (a) the improved physical environment – cleanliness of houses, yards and the community in general; (b) greatly improved health and sanitation conditions particularly the construction and use of water-sealed toilets, proper garbage disposal, increased health consciousness of the community; (c) newly learned technologies among the fishermen particularly engine repair, procedures for making better salt, and the legal aspects related to fishing; (d) more awareness among teachers/supervisors with regard to bridging the gap between community life and school learning; (e) various beneficial spin-offs from the project to the community, for example, the introduction of electricity as a result of community effort and exposure to government services. Also assistance was secured from the Ministry of Health by the mothers' club for a feeding programme for children, and participation of the community in civic-cultural programmes in the province. In brief there resulted a greater spirit of co-operation and of working towards community goals that benefit the community.

On the negative side are mentioned the following: (a) the failure of the fishpen project (largely due to lack of funds to repair damage done by two severe typhoons); (b) lack of immunization (BCG and DPT) programmes; the day care centre may eventually get to have this programme implemented, however, the service has to be provided by the Ministry of Health Regional Office; (c) gambling as a leisure-time activity has not been eradicated. All the projects could do was to introduce alternative leisure-time activities.

Overall, the participants were most appreciative of the project and ascribed many more benefits to it than the organizers and project staff did. In fact, the negative comments came from the organizers of the project rather than from the community.

Conclusion

This project illustrates the fact that for health education to succeed in a rural community that is rather isolated and which does not have the necessary amenities of urban life, the health education programme in the school cannot by itself be relied on to bring about any changes in the community unless the community itself is involved. Thus, health education becomes a programme not only for the schoolchildren but for adults in the community as well. Health topics that relate to the adult's needs and interest became the focus of the programme for this group.

The study on associations relative to health and the environment revealed that most associations were concrete, related closely to the environment, were mostly positive, that the girls more than the boys tended to give associations in the affective/psychological dimensions, and that the associations given by the English language groups related much more closely to health or the environment while the associations of the local and national language groups tended to include more of the socio-cultural, aesthetic, psychological and economic dimensions.

This experience with associations provided the teachers with a means by which to bridge the notions pupils have, their prior knowledge and attitudes, with the learning of health and science concepts in the classroom. The major change at the end of the project and a year later was the greatly improved sanitation of the community and the homes.

Reference

Hernandez D. F. (1981) Monograph 19, "The Concept of Health and Environment in Rural Communities: Two Case Studies". Science Education Center, University of Philippines. Also Monograph 35, "A Fishing Village Revisited".

26

The Agrindus Health Project

R. PREM
Banwasi Seva Ashram, UP, India

The Agrindus health project was an experiment in health education with rural, tribal people, initiated in June 1968 by the Banwasi Seva Ashram as one of the component activities of its comprehensive development programme. The approach adopted was one of "Gram Swaraj", village self-rule as described by Gandhi and Vinoba. In the philosophy of Gram Swarajya, every village is conceived as a self-reliant, self-contained community for a majority of its needs, its individuals co-operating and sharing life with each other in the belief that the welfare of every individual should be their concern and that, while exploiting nature for one's own needs, one should show respect for the environment by observing self-restraint in one's personal life.

The main objectives of the project were (1) health education of the people for healthy living and planned parenthood, (2) development of a village health service, and (3) a study of household remedies.

The project area was that of Banwasi Seva Ashram (a voluntary organization), which operates in the tribal area of the Mirzapur district in the State of UP in India. The area comprises four community development districts, 400 villages, scattered over an area of 1,114 square miles. The Ashram's activities have reached about 300 of the villages.

A survey of health and socio-economic conditions was undertaken in 13 neighbouring villages of the Ashram in the first year of the health project (1968–69). The survey revealed a great scarcity of drinking water. Food was insufficient as well as imbalanced. Housing accommodation was very poor and people suffered from diarrhoea, dysentery, chronic coughs and pains in their extremities. The main sources of employment were agriculture and the harvesting of forest produce. Agriculture was in a primitive stage and unproductive, and there was much exploitation in the harvesting of forest produce. People were caught in a vicious circle of unemployment, exploitation, poverty, malnutrition, disease and backwardness. Communication facilities in the area were meagre and literacy was only 9%. The area was already covered by the Government health

143

services, but the doctors hardly ever stayed in villages and the people depended on magic, charms, amulets, a few herbs and on indigenous medicines for the treatment of illness.

Development of the Project

The first activity was the clinic on the Ashram's premises. This was soon followed by evening visits to the neighbouring villages to explain the project. The plan of action envisaged two functioning teams, one at the village level, working part time in a voluntary capacity; and the other at the project centre, working full time for the project. About 100 village persons were to be trained for 100 villages over a period of 5 years. These persons were to initiate a dialogue on health in the community and guide the community in health care. The first batch of four primary health care persons started functioning by the end of the first year and another eight persons were trained during the next year. Their contribution was good. But thereafter it became difficult to train and involve more persons as a sufficient number of educated (middle school educated) persons was not available. Regular follow-up of the training was difficult for want of any communication facility. Inability on the part of the identified persons to be away from their homes for more than five to six days at a time made training difficult. These, and other constraints in training personnel, contributed to a re-orientation of the action plans.

The central team took over the responsibility of teaching the know-how on health to the village people by holding meetings in the villages. These meetings were possible only during the winter season, when villagers had leisure and a jeep could run on forest roads. It was soon realized that there had to be one more intermediary team to maintain a closer contact with the villagers and also to cater to their primary medical and health needs. By this time the Ashram had started six village development centres, each to serve a group of 20–30 villages. One person from the staff of each village development centre was selected for one year's training in health care at the clinic. Later more persons were trained for new village development centres. These persons received training in health know-how and primary medical care. They are called "village doctors" and are given the responsibility for health education and primary health and medical care of the community. They are in turn asked to identify enthusiastic village youths who want to know about healthy living and household remedies, and to use the knowledge in their personal life and also work for the society in a voluntary capacity. Special short-duration training courses are organized for such persons from time to time. These persons are named "Swasthya Mitra" or the "health friend". At present there are 10 village health centres and about 200 village health friends.

Continuity in learning of the whole team – on central, intermediary and village levels – is maintained by exchanging ideas and experiences at meetings, short orientation courses and conferences, held in the Ashram as well as at village health centres and in villages. A season-oriented health education and health care programme is worked out in consultation with the "village doctors". The "village doctors" in turn discuss this plan of action with the "health friends". This is followed by group meetings in the villages by the "village doctor". The village doctor's efforts are reinforced by the central team from time to time.

Audio-visual aids are used for education from time to time. Flash cards and simple pictures are found to be useful in communicating ideas. But, the most essential input is the dialogue on the subject and practice of the ideas preached. Apart from these modes of health education, health talks and short courses are organized for literacy teachers, librarians, village leaders, Ashram staff and students. Quite often, special meetings are organized for women. Reading material in the form of booklets is prepared in simple language for the use of the workers and the people in the villages.

The Achievements

A systematic evaluation of achievements has been done on three occasions to date. At the end of the second year (1970) it was observed that people placed more emphasis on education than on medical care, feeling that the former makes life better. The second evaluation, made in 1974, looked into the acceptance of the small family norm and family planning practices. It was seen that an educational approach to family planning extension was effective in introducing it, not only as a means of limiting a family, but as a way of life as evidenced by the acceptance of family planning practice by the younger age groups with only one or two children. The third evaluation is the one conducted by the Agricultural Finance Corporation of India in 1979. This evaluation covered the ideology of the Ashram and its comprehensive development programme including health. The relevant findings revealed that the literacy rate had risen from 14% to 27% and that 98% of families had benefited under the Health Programme.

The tribal population had earlier been subjected to endemic diseases and consequently to a high mortality rate, mainly because of want of proper medical aid, scarcity of food, drinking water, etc. As these facilities were made available to the project families under the programme, they made a tremendous impact on the health of the tribal people, a reduction in mortality rate, which simultaneously increased the longevity. There was also a preference in favour of a small family.

Observations made at meetings clearly indicated unqualified support for the project. A study of 622 families in 100 villages showed that the number of families benefiting from specific aspects were:

Benefit	No. of families	Percentage
Personal cleanliness	528	85%
Sanitation	127	20%
Compost making	616	99%
Safety of drinking water	436	70%
New cooking methods	302	49%
Use of oils	399	64%
Child care	156	25%
Prevention of disease	457	73%
Household remedies	321	52%

The above shows where the most benefit was observed. The low response to sanitation and child care suggests that more work is necessary on those fronts. Development is a continuous process. The experience so far is encouraging. At the same time, one thing is clear: a lot more effort is needed to reach the objective of "Health for All".

27

Health Education in Indian Villages: A New Approach

M. R. CHAKRAVARTI

Maharashtra Association for the Cultivation of Science, Pune, India

India continues to be predominantly a land of villages with living conditions almost totally unfit for most people to live and work in. Not that no efforts have been made to improve village life, but progress is slow. The Indian education system happens to be a legacy from British education, which was mainly restricted to the academic world. It has seldom been viewed as a training for life, which enables an individual to become self-reliant and self-directive in a way which is not only beneficial to the individual, but also to the community as a whole to which he belongs.

School age is the most impressionable and it is all the more important that the village school functions as the centre of activity for the furtherance of all developmental processes. Once the children recognize and value the benefit of hygiene, public health and sanitary measures, they are likely to carry forward the habits so formed into later life, thereby acting as a catalytic agent to bring about social transformation of the whole village. Hygiene cannot be built into the lifestyle of children merely by giving them take-home packets of food or packages of social welfare measures. It is much more important that children come together in their schools to play, learn and eat together – including eating together what they bring from home. In this process they learn to improve hygiene and communicate at home without any special effort. The most important factor is to appreciate that a child is born with an innate capacity to learn and it is the responsibility of the school to provide an appropriate environment as a tool for achieving a way of life more suited to our present culture, needs and resources.

Unfortunately the important task of providing adequate health education has not been given due recognition in the curriculum, but a new approach is currently being initiated in eight Maharashtra villages under the leadership of Dr. P. V. Sukhatme of the Maharashtra Association for the Cultivation of Science. The programme is planned in three phases.

Phase 1:
A wire fence is constructed around the area of the school to demarcate the campus. This is intended to provide the children with incentives to keep the campus green and clean and to use it for playing games. It has been observed that within about a year of construction and under sustained educational input, the campus presents a different picture altogether. The campus maintenance, as well as concentrating on the importance of health, becomes a part of the lifestyle.

Phase 2:
A fence is built around the well at a distance of some 30 feet from the perimeter, while simultaneously providing facilities to pump out water for storing in tanks situated outside this fence. The soil, acting as a filter, is expected to decrease materially the chance of contamination of the water with $E.$ $coli$ and other pathogenic organisms responsible for gastro-intestinal diseases.

Phase 3:
During this phase the children are encouraged to use community latrines. As they begin to use them, and get their household members to use them too, there will be a marked effect reducing morbidity.

In summary, there is interaction between the individual and the environment at all stages of this approach. The school interacts with the environment to correct malfunctioning of the ecosystem in the area surrounding the school. It also provides an opportunity for children to interact with each other outside the school in improving conditions. In brief, the school is visualized as an instrument to bring about a change in the lifestyle of the village, based on the belief that education is a process and that as the community works together under sustained stimulus, a transition takes place. In other words, an interaction between the innate educability of human beings and the environment, under the stimulus of appropriate social action, can ensure growth and development in the community.

28

Using Advertisements as a Learning Technique

H. D. THIER

Lawrence Hall of Science, University of California, USA

The purpose of all product advertising is to sell something to the buyer. This very obvious fact is frequently obscured in the sophisticated psychology used by the advertiser. For example, the purpose in showing in an advertisement a group of healthy young people smoking cigarettes on a boat or at a party is an attempt by the advertiser to associate in the buyer's mind a positive relationship between enjoying life and smoking. No matter how you feel about smoking, this is the purpose of the advertisement; yet the actual relationship between smoking and long-term enjoyment of a healthy life is proven to be negative.

With a product more useful than cigarettes such as aspirin, the advertisements are frequently overstated. For example, the pain-relieving attributes of aspirin for a headache are expanded to suggest that taking aspirin will make you a brighter, happier person. We need to help students to analyse the messages in advertisements so that they can make positive decisions about them in regard to their own health. Getting students to collect, analyse and categorize those related to health from their local media can be a valuable educational exercise by introducing them to the importance of looking carefully at evidence, as well as revealing the real purposes of many advertisements.

The activity can begin by asking the students what effect they think advertisements have on them. Bring out the idea that advertisements encourage us to buy and use products. Suggest that in order to study the relationship between advertisements and health you want each student to collect five advertisements related to health. Give a date when everyone is to have their advertisements, which can be obtained from newspapers, magazines, shops, etc. (A wise teacher will collect some as well in order to provide any student who has not brought any for one reason or another!)

When all have their five advertisements, divide the class into groups of four to discuss their twenty advertisements. Suggest they sort them into two or more categories. If necessary, help groups who need it to get started by suggesting possibilities. Hold a discussion of the categories chosen, looking at how each may affect health. For example, all advertisements in the category "sports equipment" can be considered to encourage exercise while all those in the category "sweets" to encourage overeating or poor nutrition.

When each group has had the chance to present how they sorted their advertisements (as they normally want to do), suggest that all groups sort them again into two categories. This time, however, tell them the two categories are "Those which help to improve the quality of my life" and "Those which help to destroy the quality of my life". If necessary, discuss the meaning of "quality of life" with them. For our purposes, "improving the possibilities for good health" would be an adequate explanation of the title. If groups are undecided about some advertisement, let them set up an undecided category. Whilst they are working (or beforehand) set up two places where selected advertisements can be displayed under each title. Ask each group to select two or three advertisements which they would like to display in each category. Ask them to agree on, and be ready to describe, their reasons for their selection. Encourage discussion, highlighting all ideas that indicate how the product contributes to or detracts from the quality of the user's life. Display those advertisements on which there is general agreement. Put those on which there is disagreement aside for later discussion.

Once the advertisements are displayed ask the students to discuss those in the "help to destroy" category. Ask if any of them say that the product can do harm. All advertisements tend to present the product in the most positive way, even if the product has no real benefit to the individual. In many countries cigarette advertisements have to carry a health warning: how clearly or obscurely are they shown? Highlight how advertisers try to get a harmful product to look different.

Discuss the advertisements in the "undecided" category. Emphasize the importance of everyone using the evidence which is in, and which is not in, the advertisement to make up their own mind for themselves. Many decisions which students will have to make that affect the quality of their lives will not have easy "yes" or "no" answers. It is important for them to see that frequently *how* one makes the decision is as important as the decision itself.

As a result of these activities and especially of the discussions, students should learn that:

(1) All product advertisements are intended to *sell* them something.

(2) The information presented may be incomplete, exaggerated, or even false.

(3) They need to question the claims made, using independent evidence to help them decide.

(4) There may be a more healthy way to achieve the same goal (fresh fruit instead of sweets as a source of energy, for example).

29

A CHILD-to-child Approach: A Strategy at School and Community Level

U. N. JAJOO
Sevagram, India

The majority of poor children in India do not reach secondary school education, essentially because they have to be engaged in helping their family to earn bread, perhaps by going to the fields, by driving a herd of cows or by looking after a younger child so that the mother can go to the fields.

Attempts towards "CHILD-to-child" education were planned in India (written like that as it is older children to younger children) with children in secondary schools visiting children in an urban slum or in a village once a week as a regular activity.

In the process of developing friendships, the children in school slowly realize how different the living conditions of their friends are from their own. For example, how their concept of sanitation is irrelevant in a setting where there is a lack of water, space to live in, and where the most appropriate of technology such as sanitary latrines is all beyond the reach of their friends' families; how their concept of a balanced diet is impractical in a setting where a family is fighting to make both ends meet; how protests against alcoholism and cigarette smoking get diluted within an over-whelmingly male-dominated culture in an illiterate poor setting, whether rural or urban.

The glaring revelations caused a great change in attitude among the schoolchildren. Their exposure to a live situation made them restrain voluntarily their increasing material demands. They became more and more sympathetic towards their friends. Compassion increased their commitment to the cause of the poor.

This kind of interaction between children who live in widely different circumstances is an invaluable educational means by which a child's value system may be enlightened by experiencing those of another. Anyone wishing to follow this scheme needs to work out ways of:

(a) organizing each interaction in terms of cost, travel, meeting places and times;

(b) guiding *each* participant about the aims of the interaction before it takes place;

(c) following up each interaction in order that what has been gained from it may be realized by each participant and shared by others.

30

The CHILD-to-child Approach: Health Scouts

B. YOUNG

Unicef, Nepal

In many countries of the world, older children have responsibility for looking after their younger brothers and sisters, or other younger children in their community. Recognition of this important relationship led to the establishment of the CHILD-to-child programme for the International Year of the Child in 1979. It is written "CHILD-to-child" to signify that the (older) CHILD has responsibility for a (younger) child. The programme developed many materials to be used by teachers, health workers, scout/guide leaders, youth club leaders, women's groups and others. The materials concentrate particularly on the health, welfare and general development of the younger child. They help the older children to understand their responsibilities and to show how they can contribute to shaping the future life of the little children of the family and community.

CHILD-to-child is a powerful idea. It changes the way in which we think about the teaching and learning process. It recognizes explicitly that children learn many things from each other and not only from adults. It helps children to develop emotionally by encouraging them to recognize that they have an important role to play in caring for younger children; and by giving them the knowledge and skills to fulfil that responsibility.

This responsibility can extend to general concern for the environment. Older children can act as "Health Scouts". They find out about the health resources of the community where they live; they pass on this information to their families and use the knowledge in caring for younger children.

The following is taken from an activity sheet from the CHILD-to-child programme, called Health Scouts. It is one practical example of the approach, but people can of course develop their own materials for their own context. The idea is used to best effect when it is built into school curricula and training programmes for teachers, health workers and others.

HEALTH SCOUTS

THE IDEA

A healthy community is a strong and happy one. A community is healthy when the people who live in it:

- understand what they need to be healthy;
- know what services are available and how to use them;
- care about the health of everyone else.

Children can help in making their community a better place to live in and this activity sheet shows some ways in which children can do this, for instance by:

- finding out about the health care resources in their own community;
- passing on to their families and others important health information;
- caring about the health of others, particularly children who live near them, by helping their families make the best use of available health services.

WHO COULD INTRODUCE THE ACTIVITY TO CHILDREN?

- teachers of children in the upper classes of primary schools;
- youth leaders, who can also make use of health badges in organizations that have badge schemes, such as the Boy Scouts;
- health workers and others working in community health programmes.

Teachers and health workers can plan this activity together. Parents should be told what their children are doing and why.

THE ACTIVITY

Finding out about the health needs of the community
Surveys or "find out" projects give the children practice in collecting health information and making good use of it. Children can find out about the health conditions of babies and young children in their community.

Illness and deaths from diseases like tuberculosis, diphtheria, whooping cough, tetanus, poliomyelitis and measles can be prevented if babies and young children are immunized. An important survey that children can make is to find out which children in their community have been immunized against these diseases.

Before carrying out the survey discuss with the children

- the reasons for immunization;
- which immunizations are common in your area?
- who provides them?

Perhaps a health worker could be invited to discuss this with the children.

To carry out the survey the children could make a record chart for babies and young children near them with symbols for each of the most commonly given immunizations, e.g.

BCG   – which protects against tuberculosis;
DPT   – which protects against diphtheria, whooping cough and tetanus;
Polio   – which protects against poliomyelitis;
Measles – which protects against measles.

Children can find out about children in their own families and can be made responsible for several households near them. They will need to ask parents what immunizations the children have had.

From this survey the children will have found out which babies and young children need to be immunized. Older children can tell mothers about immunization clinics and they can tell the health workers which babies need to be immunized.

Finding out about the health services available to the community
Often in a community there are many people with different kinds of health knowledge:

- some people know how to make herb teas;
- there are women who help at childbirth;
- often someone knows about first aid;
- the various trained health workers.

Where can we get help quickly and which of these people is the best one to help? This information is very useful for all of us but often we do not have it.

Children can find out about all people in their community with some special health knowledge;

- where they can be found;
- what their special health knowledge is;
- who is the best person to go to.

Discuss these things with the children and let them make a list of all the people in their community who have some special health knowledge: e.g. clinic sister, midwife, herbalist.

They can discuss their lists with each other, and decide who they should go to for the different sicknesses that occur locally.

The children can make a health services map of their community. On it they can mark where to go for help and work out the travelling time needed to get to each health helper. They can find out when and where special clinics are held.

The children could play games using their maps and asking each other, for instance, "If somebody gets burnt by the cooking fire, who will you get to help and how long will it take?"

Children can pass this information on by making a play about getting help from different people, and show it at a village meeting or on clinic days.

Telling others about health services

Children can learn to pass on health information to parents, health workers and others, e.g.:

- Children can "adopt" a newborn baby in the family or community, and make a vaccination card to remind the mother when the baby is due to be immunized.
- Health workers can tell the school when they are to hold a clinic in the village, and school children can visit homes in the area the day before the clinic to tell families the correct time and place. Each child can be responsible for telling several households.
- Each older child can be a health leader for a few households, and tell the health worker where help is needed, or pass on information from the health worker to the household.

Helping to care for the health of others

There are many ways in which children can help in looking after the health of other children. For example, they can become helpers at the health clinic. Teachers and health workers would need to plan this together, but some ways in which children can help are:

- weighing babies and filling in charts;
- organizing play groups for children waiting with their mothers. Toys and games could be made and brought along to amuse young children;
- acting as interpreter for mothers and health workers, to pass on instructions for feeding programmes or treatments;
- helping to cook at feeding demonstrations;
- helping to clean up at the clinic.

Other ways for older children to be health helpers might be to:

- run simple first aid clinics at school;

- make toys and games for child minders;
- prepare food for younger children at school;
- bring young children to the clinic;
- "adopt" a younger child in the school and notice when they are sick or need treatment for sores;
- make health posters and notices.

Other activities for children
Other surveys which children can carry out:

- find out where diseases occur in the area. Then pass on the information to health workers, or use it as a basis for a health campaign. Why have the patients been sick or had an accident in the past year? What sickness did they have? What time of the year was it? How often did they have it?
- find out about local medicine; what plants are used? Who knows how to make up the medicine? When is it used?

Many other free-activity sheets are available from the address given below. They include the following which give some idea of the range of topics which can be approached through CHILD-to-child:

Shakir Strip
Our Babies Growing Up
Playing with Younger Children
Toys and Games
More Healthy Food
Care of Children with Diarrhoea
Our Teeth
Health Scouts
Our Neighbourhood
Accidents
Handicapped Children
Understanding Children's Feelings
Looking after Eyes
Let's Find Out How Well Children See and Hear
Caring for Children Who Are Sick
Early Signs of Illness
A Place to Play
Helping the Severely Deaf Child
Growing Vegetables in Containers
The Management of Little Children's Stools

A series of readers about health matters, written in simple English, a general introductory book to CHILD-to-child, and handbooks on "CHILD-to-child and the disabled", and "CHILD-to-child in refugee camps" are also available. Many materials have been translated into other languages (French, Arabic and Spanish) and many more have been adapted to suit particular contexts and circumstances.

For more information, write to:
CHILD-to-child
Institute of Child Health
30 Guildford Street
LONDON WC1N 1EH, UK

31

Two Health Education Projects from the Lawrence Hall of Science

H. THIER

Lawrence Hall of Science, University of California, USA

At the Lawrence Hall of Science we have developed and are developing a wide variety of instructional programmes concerned with the societal implications of science. The following two examples, in particular, focus on individuals' decision-making regarding their personal health and lifestyle, and how they participate as members of the community with regard to the issues raised.

The Health Activities Project (HAP)

The emphasis here is on science-based experiences related to the individual's own health and lifestyle. Emphasized is the concept that, based on evidence, you can take control of your own lifestyle and, therefore, improve the quality of your personal health. HAP, a cooperative project between the Lawrence Hall of Science and the Association of Science and Technology Centers (ASTC) has developed materials useful in the schools and science centres nationwide. Funding for this instructional innovation came from the Robert Wood Johnson Foundation and this was one of the first instances of private foundation support for such a programme.

It involves students with their own health and safety through hands-on, discovery approach activities. By investigating their own bodies, the students learn at first hand how their bodies function, what their bodies can do and, most importantly, that they can make changes in the way their bodies perform. The project's main purpose is to make students more aware of the control they have over their own health and safety.

It is a science-based student-centred health curriculum programme. The

161

hands-on discovery approach is utilized to enhance understanding of concepts and to increase peer interaction. Some individual activities include: students comparing the work load of different exercises by measuring their own pulse rates; making plaster impressions of their teeth to gain a better understanding of the arrangement and function of their teeth; wearing particle masks and adhesive strips to monitor the air for dirt and dust; playing a board game in which they try to balance their food intake with exercises; designing their own advertisements based on some of the hidden appeals in health product advertisements.

The activities are designed primarily to supplement and enrich existing school programmes in health, physical education and science, but the complete HAP programme can also be used as a comprehensive health curriculum. Some of the activities can also be used with a variety of other subjects including social science, mathematics and music. The original project was directed primarily at 10–15-year-olds. Currently the HAP staff is working on additional materials for youngsters 5–8 years old.

The "Risk and Youth: Smoking" programme (RAY:S)

The purpose of the RAY:S programme is to prevent young adolescents from beginning to smoke now or in the future and to reduce the number of youngsters who presently smoke cigarettes.

It is the product of the three-year study funded by the National Cancer Institute. The study developed a theoretical model to explain why some adolescents resist smoking, while others take up "the habit". It was based on research involving over 10,000 students in the San Francisco Bay area. Based on this model and extensive classroom trials by project staff, the RAY:S material was developed, revised and prepared for field testing. The results of the field trials in the spring of 1982 showed that the curriculum was effective in curtailing smoking behaviour in young adolescents.

The project is an example of the use of science-based instruction to attack the problem of cigarette smoking, which has been described as "the single most important preventable environmental factor contributing to illness, disability and death in the United States".

The material provides a self-contained curriculum for students in the upper elementary and junior high schools in the USA. It comprises nine core activity sessions plus one evaluation session. Complementary optional activities are also included to challenge inquisitive students. The smoking-related subject areas explored in the curriculum include:

– Temptations to smoke
– The nature of addiction
– Physiological effects of smoking
– The tobacco industry and its advertising efforts

- Peer and societal influences on decision-making and problem-solving for teen-age students
- The rights of smokers and non-smokers
- The efforts made by the cigarette industry to attract people between the ages of 12 and 18 years to smoke.

The curriculum encourages students to question, research independently and make informed decisions on the vital issues surrounding smoking. Some examples of the activities are as follows:

SESSION	DESCRIPTION	ACTIVITY
1. You, your temptations and smoking	Students consider situations which may tempt them to smoke a cigarette	Each student completes a "tempting situations" self test
3. Cigarettes will mess you up!	Students examine the immediate physiological effects of smoking	Students observe the smoking of a cigarette and discuss their observations
6. Who wants teens to smoke?	Students investigate the advertising strategies of tobacco manufacturers	Students examine and interpret a report investigating tobacco manufacturers' advertising campaigns, and compare "public" and confidential versions
9. The Long Ride Home – an unfinished drama	Students explore possible methods of resolving conflict by co-operation and compromise	Students complete the second act of a two-act play which deals with smoker and non-smoker rights

Further information about both these programmes can be obtained from the author at the Lawrence Hall of Science, University of California, Berkeley, CA 94720, USA.

The common factor in both of these examples is the emphasis on using experience-based science as an approach for building increased awareness, knowledge and understanding in young people regarding issues of high concern to them as individuals and as members of society as a whole. By concentrating on the science rather than emotionalism and rhetoric, both of these projects are able to affect decisions without appearing biased or representing one special interest group. At the same time the activities themselves teach young people basic science and, as important, how to approach problems and issues from a scientific point of view.

Our experience in developing and disseminating these materials indicates clearly that such a focus on societal issues increases dramatically student interest in learning science and teacher interest in teaching it.

32

A Teaching Unit on Population

Y. SAPIR, D. CHEN and R. NOVIK

Tel Aviv University, Israel

The following instructional unit exemplifies the integration of various aspects of health within the framework of science teaching. The starting point is a science- and technology-related societal issue. The science aspect focuses on the laws of natural phenomena and processes. The technological aspect focuses on intervention of humans in natural processes and the development of various means for fulfilling their needs. The social aspect illuminates the social and moral implications of applying science and technology.

The unit deals with the dynamics of plant, animal and human population growth as a background for understanding the problem of the growth of human populations, its origin and possible solution. Whereas natural control mechanisms serve to balance the size of plant and animal populations, the development of medicine and technology has interfered with natural control and the balancing processes of human population growth. Thus we get a huge increase in the rate of growth of the world's human population.

The unit is interdisciplinary, integrating biological and demographic concepts related to zoology, botany, geography, statistics and health sciences. Such an interdisciplinary approach requires teaching using a variety of skills, including methods of pure scientific enquiry, decision-making, strategies for value assessment, problem-solving, all of which should equip the student with the ability to face problems with social implications.

The Structure of the Content

This is illustrated in the flow chart, which shows the main themes in the unit. The *scientific* aspect covers the basic laws of population dynamics in all organisms.

- The reproduction capacity: the capacity in plants to generate seeds and to sprout; the number of births in animals, and the number of eggs laid; the number of births in humans.
- Survival of young organisms: the relationship between the number of sprouting seeds and the developing plants; the number of eggs which were laid and the hatching animals; the number of young born and those that survive.
- Death rate: death rate in animals; the proportion of people who die because of natural disasters or as the result of the activities of humans.

The unit also deals with statistical concepts related to the above factors, such as natural growth, life expectancy and birth and death rates.

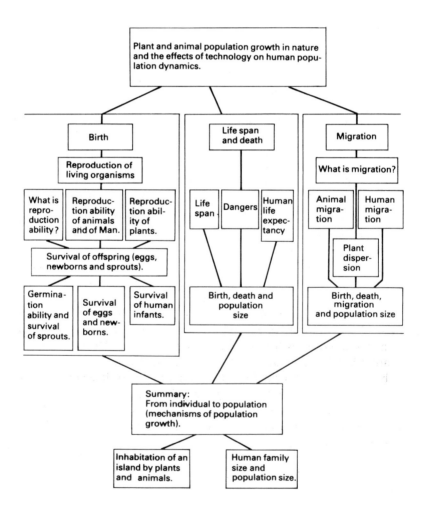

The major problem to be discussed focuses attention on the difference between mankind and other living organisms. How is it that human beings, whose reproduction ability is relatively low, have become a predominant species among mammals, whereas plants and animals with much greater reproduction ability do not overcrowd the world? In order to reach a solution the pupil becomes acquainted with the various factors influencing the size of plant and animal populations, and those affecting human population size. Three major determinants of population size are dealt with: birth, death and migration.

Learning is organized in two planes with regard to each of the above factors. The first concerns phenomena and processes (in different disciplines) which are important for the understanding of various aspects of the three above-mentioned factors, as well as their influence on population growth. The other deals with the interaction of these three factors, which determines the population size, which is expressed by calculation of natural growth balance (birth and death) and immigration balance.

The answer to the major problem presented by the Unit, is derived through analysis of the factors affecting population size, in which special emphasis is put on the uniqueness of Man. The rate of death of both young and old organisms in nature prevents crowding; Man, on the other hand, has developed technical means to reduce the rate of death, thus increasing the rate of population growth.

The *technological* aspect emphasizes the uniqueness of Man as compared with other organisms. It describes Man's interference in natural processes and the changes of balance this has brought about; Man's ability to influence the size of the population and the quality and standard of living of individuals, which is unparalleled by any other living creature; various means of child care and hygiene are considered as necessities for maintaining the health of the population, as are technological advances in the cure and prevention of disease.

The *social* aspects focus on the implications of the various scientific and technological aspects introduced in the unit. The critical importance which birth rate, infant mortality and human life expectancy play in shaping the character of society is emphasized. Underdeveloped countries are characterized by high birth rate, high death rate and low life expectancy, whereas the opposite is true for developed countries. The social implications are related to a great extent to health and medicine. The discussion contributes to the understanding of the importance of hygiene, as well as the place of medical services in serving the community.

The social-cultural context of the scientific and technological issues provides a relevant framework for discussing central issues which impinge on contemporary society.

PART V

Psychological Aspects

Introduction

This section focuses on the psychological aspects of health education. It is assumed that mental health is a continuum between pathological states and a dynamic realization of full mental health. It is also accepted that the mental health of the individual is closely interconnected with somatic and social health and furthermore to the "health" of the cultural and natural environment in which the individual operates.

The continuum can be visualized as follows:

Mental disease   Complete mental health in
Mental sickness   A   B   C   the sense of creative self-
                                                           realization

Mental health education needs to be relevant to the three points indicated on this continuum. At A, teachers should be able to recognize and refer health problems perceived in pupils. This depends on practical courses on child psychology and child psychiatry during initial and in-service training.

At B on the continuum, prevention is possible by teachers if psychological competence is enlarged and coping skills are acquired. This requires an appreciation of risk factors and an understanding of stress, and these are discussed in the first paper in this section by L. M. Bouter.

The idea of holistic, complete health, as indicated at C, is utopian. This should be looked on as a direction of development. In most cultures there will be much overlap with spiritual and religious ideals. It is important to emphasize, both explicitly and implicitly, that individuals may differ a great deal with respect to the general concept of mental health. Insight into this aspect of mental health is conveyed by example and it is through example that parents, teachers and peers have important impact on the mental well-being of pupils.

After the first paper, there is an interesting paper outlining a programme for teachers organized by the National Institute of Mental Health and Neurosciences in Bangalore, and this is followed by an example of a resource for mental health education from the same source.

33

Psychosomatic Aspects of Health: Their Relevance to Education

L. M. BOUTER
University of Limbirg, The Netherlands

A thorough insight into the causes of health problems is an important aspect of health education. At present, a multifactorial aetiology is generally taken as a starting point. In this aetiology ill-health results from a complex interaction of factors. Health-menacing factors are often referred to as risk factors. The presence of such a risk factor does not necessarily result in the occurrence of health problems. Often the health problem is dependent on the presence or absence of other factors.

Risk factors can be roughly divided into three groups. The *first group* consists of risk factors that originate in the material environment. Bacteria, viruses, chemical substances and radiation are the most important ones in this group. Infections and deficiency diseases are closely (but not exclusively) related to these factors. The *second group* is usually referred to as lifestyle. This concerns the individual's behaviour, and personal habits with regard to smoking, drinking, food and physical exercise. Risk factors in this group appear to be closely related to the most important causes of death in the industrialized countries, namely, cardiovascular diseases and cancer. The *third group* of risk factors is comprised of various psychosocial stressors. It is this group of risk factors especially which is referred to when psychosomatic diseases are discussed. These are diseases associated with abnormal physiological changes in organs that are innervated by the autonomous nervous system, and influenced by events in the environment that have a menacing psychological relevance.

The classical psychosomatic disorders such as peptic ulcers, migraine, asthma, eczema, low back pain, or psoriasis fall into this category. It is known, however, that in many other diseases such as influenza, cardio-vascular diseases, multiple sclerosis and cancer, psychosomatic processes are relevant to the aetiology and the prognosis of the disease. Besides these somatic consequences of an overload psychosomatic stress, there might certainly also develop mental or mixed somatic and mental health problems. Those are kept outside the discussion in this chapter.

Alternatively, one could make a distinction between risk factors which are (potentially) under the control of the individual and those which are not. School health education is mainly concerned with the first category. It aims at controlling risk factors and in this way focuses attention on the promotion of health. However, the modifying of the environment might also be considered a task of the health educator, especially when the coping possibilities are very limited. But this comes outside the domain of health education lessons.

Although the precise influence of psychosocial stress on the originating of disease is not at all clear, yet it seems beyond doubt that the presence or absence of psychosocial stress, and especially the individual's ability or disability to deal with it, have important consequences for his health, both in a positive and in a negative sense. It is for this reason that it is important to pay attention to the recognition of, and the dealing with, psychosocial stress in health education in schools.

At this point it should be made clear that psychosocial stress cannot be a sufficient cause of disease on its own. It must be looked upon as an element of a cluster of risk factors. Sometimes it is a very crucial element, on the road to health problems, sometimes it is not, depending on other contributing risk factors.

The Stress Mechanism

The word stress has predominantly negative meaning in everyday speech. Stress mostly refers to the pressure the individual experiences in his social environment: stress on the road, stress on the job, and stress at school. Moreover, the word stress usually implies a direct reference to its supposed negative result such as over-excitement, ulcers and heart attacks. From a biological point of view, however, the stress mechanism represents a valuable adaptation of the organism to its environment. The introduction of the word stress in its present meaning is usually attributed to the physiologist Seyle. He found that experimental animals reacted according to a stereotype physiological reaction pattern when they were submitted to threatening situations such as electrical shocks and swimming in cold water for a long period of time. This reaction enables the organism to react fast to sudden danger with fight or flight.

For human beings the stress reaction appears to be an important element in interaction with the environment in which physiological as well as psychosocial aspects can be distinguished:

- an environmental component: the stress source ("stressor");
- an interpretative component: the interpretation of the situation as threatening ("appraisal");
- a behavioural component: the individual reacts according to a personal style ("coping");
- a bodily component: the physiological stress-reaction ("strain").

In this interactional approach, environmental influences do not necessarily have to induce a stress reaction. The way in which the individual interprets the situation ("appraisal") and deals with it ("coping") is of crucial importance. The aspects "appraisal" and "coping" represent the extent to which psychological stress can be looked upon as a risk factor potentially controllable by the individual. The physiological aspects of the stress reaction ("strains") consist of changes in the autonomous functions in the organism that are induced via the autonomic nervous system and the hormone system. The target organs of these "stress hormones" are in particular the heart and blood-vessels, the central nervous system, the immune system, the digestive system and the musculature. In principle these physiological changes enable the organism to react rapidly and adequately to sudden changes. The positive effects of the stress reaction stop, however, when the balance between carrying-capacity and burden has been disturbed drastically and/or for a prolonged period of time, and if the situation is less often experienced by the individual as challenging and more often as threatening. In that case the adaptive value of the stress reaction diminishes severely and the health-threatening effects of the "strains" tend to dominate. Biologically speaking one could assume that the revolutionary cultural changes in the last twenty thousand years went much too fast to enable genetic adaptation of this originally life-saving mechanism.

These situations of chronic and severe acute stress are often connected with certain syndromes, the so-called psychosomatic diseases. In this an important problem is that of specificity. To answer the question why one person will get an ulcer when he is experiencing psychosocial stress, while another will develop a heart disease and a third one will remain perfectly healthy, various hypotheses have been developed. Psychosomatic aetiology has been thought to be related to specific personalities, to attitudes, to emotions, and a more recent approach is the "social learning" model.

In this model the line of argument goes as follows. Some situations in the environment are physically and psychologically threatening to such a degree that they are acting as severe stressors for almost anyone and are injurious to health. Examples of this are working at an extreme high pace, life-threatening war situations, and important incidents in the personal sphere, the so-called "life-events". Circumstances in daily life are usually less extreme. Psychological processes and learning processes in the past play a crucial role in the reaction to the complex and often ambiguous stressors in everyday life.

Consequently, there are remarkable differences in physiological stress-reactions ("strains") in relation to the amount of threat that is perceived by the individual ("appraisal") and to the way in which he reacts ("coping"). Psychosocial stressors that can be found are role uncertainty, role conflicts, helplessness, chronic under- and over-stimulation, and the absence of social support.

The influence of psychosocial stressors is heavily dependent on the individual's perception of success in dealing with certain situations ("coping") and the degree of control he or she possesses, or thinks he or she possesses over the situation. Predictability of unpleasant situations and feedback regarding the effectiveness of the strategies for dealing with them are important factors. The degree to which one is aware of the physiological changes which are induced by the "stress hormones" in the body, is also strongly determining for the experienced stress. Another important factor in determining the individual's capacity to withstand psychosocial stress, is the social support that is perceived from the family, relatives, friends, and at work. In general, the widely divergent recommendations that are made in the literature in relation to stress-reduction and prevention link up closely with one or more of the aforementioned aspects of the stress reaction.

Stress and Education

From the above it will be clear that psychosocial stress is an integral and moreover necessary constituent of human existence. In education one can distinguish three groups of potential stressors.

First, there is the psychosocial stress that is related to a particular period in the lives of the pupils (early youth, puberty or adolescence). The discovery of their own bodies, sexuality and identity often causes insecurity and anxiety. Along with the growing awareness of their own bodies there is usually a rising tendency to experience dissatisfaction and tension as physical symptoms. It is plausible that if no adequate strategies are developed by the individual to deal with the experienced stressors ("coping"), this might lead to a lasting psychosomatic symptomatology. A developing insight into the personal physiological functioning and the extension of coping-abilities are therefore important items for health education in schools.

The *second group* of potential stressors is embodied in the educational system itself. With this, the problem is whether it would be better to change the system in such a way that harmful stressors will disappear, or whether attempts should be made to teach the individual how to deal with situations in more adequate ways. This is dependent on personal opinions about society and education, the degree to which the potential stressor is actually active, and the assessment of the potential to change the situation.

Pressure of time, frequent changes in physical environment, changes in classmates and teachers, noise annoyance, feelings of impotence, anxiety over tests and exams, negative future perspectives (unemployment, etc) are mentioned as system-dependent stressors. The acknowledgement and development of the ability to discuss these potential stressors, as well as an exploration of the possibilities for "changing" and "dealing" strategies in the classroom situation are contributions of health education here.

A *third cluster* of psychosocial stressors is formed by the circumstances that make the profession of the teacher a stress-filled sphere of activity. A psychosomatic symptomatology specifically connected with teaching may be considered. In the past few years, quite a number of publications on the "burnout-syndrome" of teachers, "teacher-anxiety" and the "mid-life crisis" in education have been published. The large number of pupils per class, disciplinary problems, disturbed relations with colleagues, lack of professional knowledge, along with advancing age, a widening generation gap with the pupils, lack of career opportunities, lack of influence on the form and content of education, are mentioned as explanations of the high frequency of psychosomatic complaints among teachers. It should be clear that individual appraisal of the situation also plays a crucial role. In relation to these potential stressors, the problem of adaptation of either the individual or the environment presents itself. On a limited scale courses in stress management especially designed for teachers are being organized. Attention to stress prevention in initial teacher training courses and in continuation courses seems to be extremely important for both teachers and pupils.

Besides the motives for paying attention to stress prevention and management in education that have been listed above, another important reason to deal with the stress-mechanism in health education has to be mentioned. This consideration is of a didactic nature.

The stress model offers more than any other approach a conceptual framework for understanding the idea that psychological phenomena deeply influence the physical functioning of the body and eventually may cause functional changes in it. The stress model is attractive since it is biologically (adaptation to possible threats), and in particular neuro-endocrinologically (changes in the entire organism caused by the "stress-hormones") plausible. By explaining in simple terms how psychological processes affect the physiological functioning, the relation between body (soma) and mind (psyche) can be made the subject of discussion at a very basic level. In this sense theorizing about stress and psychosomatics contributes to the realization of a post-Cartesian image of human beings which seems to be of importance to health education.

Lessons on Stress

Starting from the premise that health education in schools is desirable, it is necessary to discuss in what way this may be achieved. Within the scope of this chapter it is impossible to enter into the content of actual lessons, because this will depend on the age of the pupils, the type of education and the time available. Therefore we will restrict ourselves to a discussion of the main principles.

Although it is obviously out of the question (and, hopefully, unnecessary as well) to perform professional therapy in the classroom, an important part of the lesson will be to offer perspectives on stress management and prevention, and of course some intervention by the teacher may be useful. It must be emphasized that besides explicit lessons on stress management and prevention, the ambience in the school must be conducive towards the development of a coping potential in pupils. This is by no means an attempt to open the flood gates of the anti-stress industry. It is quite unnecessary to entangle with bio-feedback, desensitization, reattribution, hypnosis, yoga, transcendental meditation or cry-therapy. Nor can a standard recipe to deal with stress be offered. Starting from the theoretical concept of "stress" inoculation, there are ideally three stages to be dealt with in lessons as discussed below.

Stress inoculation starts with the principle of the interactional model of stress defined above and aims foremost at the valuation ("appraisal") of and dealing ("coping") with a particular personal situation. Emphasis should be put on encouraging pupils to regard stress-filled situations as problems which can be solved. Changes with respect to behaviour, self-regulating activity and cognitive structures are aimed at. Non-adaptive behaviour is identified as such and replaced by behaviour which reduces the stress reaction. By using selfregulating activity the aim is especially geared towards reducing feelings of helplessness, fear, depression, self-denial and fatalism. Changes in cognitive structures concern mostly the usual implicit presumptions and assumptions about an individual's inter-action with the environment. It will be clear that targets have to be set with moderation, that the elaboration will be different for each pupil, and that the results will have to be considered with modesty.

The first phase of the "stress course" which we have in mind is the *conceptual* or *cognitive phase*. In this phase the stress reaction will be explained and it will be pointed out how stress may become a problem. Emphasis will be put on the fact that in any person's life various specific stressors can be active, and on the importance of insight into these stressors. By way of exercises and interviews, the individual determinants of a stress reaction will be clarified as far as possible. The main targets are an enlargement of analytic abilities, an awareness of personal limits, and an awareness of circumstances in which the dealing strategies prove to be insufficient. For practical reasons it is advisable to confine oneself to a limited number of stressors that occur frequently in any particular period in a pupil's life. Exercises in which an ordering of stress-filled situations is made might be useful.

The second stage is focused on an extension of the *strategies for dealing with stress* ("coping") in order to encourage flexible reactions. Instrumental skills such as communication techniques, learning skills, decision procedures or ways to avoid the stressor, will be dealt with. Also the so-called "palliative skills" such as the seeking of social support, relaxation, the expression of emotions, partial or complete denial, or concentration improvement are of importance. It is essential to emphasize that there are no standard good or bad solutions, but each strategy may prove to be valuable in certain situations for certain individuals. In classroom situations, the most feasible is the use of relaxation and concentration exercises. Exercises for muscle relaxation and an inventory of early individual physical symptoms seem to be feasible assignments for self-activity.

Application is the third and last phase of stress inoculation. The aim is to increase confidence in newly acquired coping skills. As has been mentioned before, perception of control over a difficult situation is crucial with respect to stress reaction. This session is one in which experiences with application will be shared and discussed. It will be evident that the approach that has been described above, will need further elaboration, especially regarding the various types of education, and the effects of an approach like this will have to be evaluated thoroughly. However, the (limited) research that has been done in this field justifies moderate optimism.

Conclusion

Psychosocial stress is a necessary factor in life and a risk factor for a large number of diseases. This makes the signalizing of, and the coping with psychosocial stress important items with regard to health. In early youth, puberty and adolescence, experiments with all kinds of behaviour are made. Since these experiments also concern behaviour that is related to health, the basis for a future illness-carrier, as far as this is determined by behavioural factors, is made. The stages in life which have been mentioned are also important for learning how to cope with psychosocial stress and possibly evoked physiological phenomena ("strains").

Management and prevention of stress are important in health education in schools. The enlargement of "coping skills", a cognitive reorganization of the experiencing of stressors ("appraisal") and their application in situations where stress actually occurs ("transfer") are the main aspects of an effective approach. This certainly implies also that schools should not be overprotective towards their pupils.

34

School Mental Health: A Programme for Teachers

M. KAPUR and S. SRINATH

National Institute of Mental Health and Neurosciences, Bangalore, India

Involving teachers in mental health aspects of children is an important part of education. It is especially necessary in third world countries where the provision of any kind of health care is almost non-existent. The National Institute of Mental Health and Neurosciences in Bangalore has been actively engaged since 1975 in implementing a variety of innovative programmes and evaluating their efficacy. One was to train school teachers in the early detection and management of mental health problems amongst children. This programme involved 250 teachers from nine schools over a period of 9 years and covered approximately 15,000 children. It was concerned with schools over the whole socio-economic strata, including residential schools and schools for the physically handicapped.

Certain prerequisites were necessary for the effective functioning of the programme. In spite of the heavy burden on a teacher (a heavy teaching schedule, crowded classrooms, etc), it was important to generate interest in helping distressed children and a willingness to cross the usual barriers of teacher/student relationships to get closer to the children. Participation by the teachers in the programme was voluntary without extra incentives, monetary or otherwise.

The first phase was orientation of the teachers in five weekly sessions of 1½ hours in groups of 20–30. The content dealt with:

(1) causes of problems with an emphasis on the many factors involved;

(2) disorders of emotion, such as being extremely shy, withdrawn, over-anxious or depressed;

(3) disorders of conduct, such as lying, stealing and repeated truancy;

(4) specific problems of specific groups, such as school refusal in the younger child, or adolescent adjustment in the older age group;

(5) poor school performance, the most common complaint with which teachers and parents are concerned;

EH–G

(6) psychosomatic problems with asthma, obesity, etc, serious mental illnesses like psychoses, epilepsy and consequent disturbances in school performance.

In this first phase, teachers are taught to recognize those cases which need to be referred and where they should be referred.

The second phase aims at training those teachers who are interested in managing problem cases themselves. This is done in 20 or more weekly sessions of 1½ hours each for small closed group of 8–10 teachers. It aims at training the teachers in the management of cases which do not require referral to a specialist and can be effectively handled in school. Actual care of children is involved in the course and there are visits to child guidance clinics, etc.

Some of the results encountered are as follows. The more experienced and older the teachers, the greater is their sensitivity to the issues discussed by comparison with younger inexperienced teachers, who may have acquired their theoretical knowledge too early in their teaching careers. There is often an over-expectation in terms of eventual outcomes from the school authorities and teachers. It was learnt that bureaucratic tangles can delay a whole programme!

Experience has shown that reluctant heads and unenlightened colleagues are not conducive to setting up counselling services within schools. It is very necessary to generate interest in the entire school set-up. To sum up, the experience has shown that it is feasible to get teachers to recognize and even intervene when faced with problems pertaining to mental health.

Reflections

The above account may suggest the programme was an educative experience for the teachers involved. But to be honest, it has been an intensely gratifying and highly educative experience for the authors of the programme as well.

Education is an experience which can be effective only if the educators are committed to what is being taught and care about those they teach. They have to earn trust before the information they impart can be trusted. Of course, there are always reasons to be wary of information givers, and the educator has to have a high regard for the common sense of those to be taught and the ability to choose what will be suitable for them, as it is only then that what is imparted will be assimilated.

The programme was compiled on the basis of the experience of the authors. We come from a cultural background which is undergoing a lot of changes by its openness to the influences impinging on it by the advances in technology, but there is one bastion still defended, that is the protection of children. The degree of freedom given to children in India is much less than that in the liberal attitudes in the West. It is apparent that extremes are wrong, but in our Indian culture high orthodoxy can be a stumbling block in the attempts of a child to grow into his or her own person. For the benefit of any educator wanting to bring about change in others, we should like to quote one of the teachers who successfully worked, in tremendous adversity, with adolescents from extremely deprived backgrounds, with very little gratitude from parents and in fact often actual rebuff. Having endured one such rebuff from a father, the teacher concerned was asked how he could continue under such circumstances. He calmly replied: "It has to be done. If we do not do it, who will?" This perhaps is the essence of effective education; it represents the highest ethical values, leading to right judgement, leading in turn to right action.

References

1. A Manual on Child Mental Health and Psychosocial Development. Part III for the school teachers. Graham, Jegede, Kapur, Minde, Nikapota, Sell. W.H.O., Regional Office for South East Asia, New Delhi, India (1982).
2. An orientation course for school teachers. Malavika Kapur and Illana Cariapa. *Indian Journal of Clinical Psychology* **6**, 75–80 (1978).
3. Training in counselling for school teachers. Malavika Kapur and Illana Cariapa. *International Journal for the Advancement of Counselling* **2**, 109–115 (1979).
4. Mental health problems amongst school children. Malavika Kapur, Shiv Prakash and Parthasarathy. School Science NCERT Publication. *A Journal of Education* **xix**, 1 (March 1981).
5. Child Mental Health Problems (Guide to school teachers). Child guidance clinic. National Institute of Mental Health and Neurosciences, Bangalore-560029, India.

35

An Example of a Resource Syllabus for Mental Health Education

Devised by M. Kapur and S. Srinath for use in a rural community

A. What is Life?

Birth.→Body growth.→Independence.→ Old age.————→Death.
 Learning. Managing one's Wisdom. Loss of
 own affairs. Body weakness. body
 Complementary Dependence. form.
 role of men and Unity with
 women. mass of
 Family life as universe.
 co-operative
 enterprise.

B. What is Living?

1. Attaining maturity Body –the body's capacity to cater for one's own
 needs and for reproduction.
 Mind –acquiring knowledge of surroundings, of
 social behaviour and of fulfilling one's own
 needs.
2. Learning skills for catering to one's needs.
3. Use of the knowledge and skills gained.
4. Sense, creativity, individuality and happiness.
5. Understanding the universe through experience of living – acquiring
 wisdom.
6. Transfer of knowledge to younger generation.

C. What are Special Needs?

A CHILD
- is ignorant of environment, needs guidance and protection,
- cannot manage its own affairs, needs care and guidance,
- needs encouragement and appreciation in learning and self-help,
- wants recognition and respect,
- expects love, care and respect from those in close contact.

These needs are fulfilled in joint families. Parents have less time and patience, but grandparents have leisure, patience and experience in child care.

AN ADOLESCENT
- is developing ideas for shaping personality and future,
- is still learning skills for earning livelihood and dealing with society,
- has little grasp of total life,
- needs associates.

Parents and grandparents need to develop friendship and relationships so that adolescent is protected against exploitation in society and is helped to find real associates in creativity.

A YOUNG MAN/ WOMAN
- is enthusiastic about living,
- is adventurous, feels confident of shaping their lives in accordance with their likings,
- has less patience and tolerance, gets easily upset,
- needs psychological support, love, care, respect, appreciation.

Marriage (unifying separate identities) provides the necessary strength. Elders provide hope and guidance.

AN OLD MAN/ WOMAN
- has wisdom, but physical capacities are reduced,
- needs care and expects respect for past efforts. Nuclear family can provide the care and can benefit from their wisdom and help in child care, and from their encouragement.

D. What are the Difficulties in Living?

1. Needs are many and varied and difficult to meet single-handed.
2. It is a hurdle race rather than smooth-running.
3. One often meets with unexpected, unprecedented events of significance.
4. Need to be vigilant, learning to adapt and to mould.
5. Tolerate and be patient, be hopeful, keep on going!

E. What Helps in Living?

1. Mutual co-operation and complementation.
2. Making a nuclear family – husband, wife and children – offering a fulfilment of basic needs with some ease.
3. Having a joint family with grandparents – offering, in addition to the above, guidance and psychological support and easy child care.
4. Concern for neighbours and co-operation with them – sharing of life – giving strength and support in overcoming difficulties in personal and social life.
5. Concern for community, an extension of family feeling:
   - possibility of division of labour
   - ease of working
   - improvement in efficiency
   - strength to face natural calamities
   - strength to face aggression, etc
   - strength to adapt to new situations
   - enriches life,
   - fulfils basic needs,
   - promotes art and culture,
   - provides respect,
   - reduces violence,
   - increases happiness.
6. Concern for surroundings – care of natural resources, neatness, avoiding waste – contributes to health and to the permanence of life's resources.

F. What Helps in Facing the Realities of Life?

An understanding of the following:
- things take time to take shape,
- mistakes can be made in understanding, in learning and doing, and so there may be failures,
- at times failures are due to jealousy and to the selfish influence of others,
- at times they are due just to chance,
- achievement is due to the harmonious action of more than one influencing factor, an individual being one of them,

- no experience is lasting – hence there is no need to be frustrated and to grumble,
- difficulties and failures provide opportunities for adventure and for new creation,
- contentment comes from right deeds, they are contributions to well-being,
- material things possessed offer only short-lasting happiness,
- an understanding of life in its totality offers long-lasting happiness.

36
Analysing Pupils' Problems

In order to be able to deal with a pupil's problems in school, it is important to take into consideration as many causes of the problem as possible. It was suggested that the following might be helpful in diagnosing causes of problems. By analysing the behaviour of the child carefully, an appropriate strategy for treatment can be adopted.

Possible causes of poor performance in school

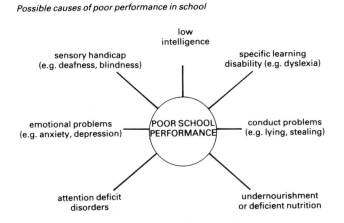

Possible causes of an over-active child in class

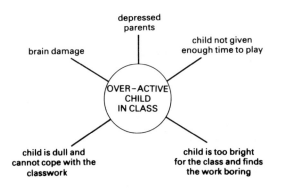

EH–G*

PART VI

Decision-making and Ethics

Introduction

In recent years there has been a movement in many parts of the world, which is now gaining more and more momentum, to incorporate social, economic and environmental issues into the teaching of science. It is, of course, particularly relevant to health education. This trend has the advantage of showing students the relevance of what is being taught, which helps to make it more meaningful, and this often results in increased motivation to pursue studies further. Inevitably incorporating such issues raises ethical aspects and involves students in decision-making. These are usually matters which students find profoundly interesting and experience has shown that raising them in the context of science teaching leads to lively and stimulating sessions. However it must be accepted that this kind of teaching is new to most teachers of science and there is an understandable reluctance on the part of many teachers to embark on a journey into new territory for which they were not trained.

The first paper in this section indicates some ethical topics which are relevant to health, and the second paper describes techniques which can be used for dealing with such topics in the classroom.

A paper by Valerie Payne on population as an issue is followed by an example of the use of a decision-making simulation exercise in which the issues involved in setting up a health service in a developing country promote thought about the rival claims of prevention and cure in such a service. A final paper by Margaret Brumby describes in detail an issue associated with organ transplants.

37
Teaching Ethical Aspects of Health Care

M. BRUMBY and V. PAYNE

Listed below are some examples of topics which can provide an opportunity for students and younger pupils to examine the values which they have concerning health care.

The Cow

In a village there was a family with six children. The children were seen not to be getting enough food. A health worker arranged for the family to get a cow, so that the milk could be given to the children.

Some weeks later the health worker visited and found the children had made no improvement. She investigated and found that the father was selling the milk for grain so that he could feed the whole family, instead of giving the milk just to his children.

What should the health visitor do?

Hospitals or Rural Health Centres?

The government of Marimbia, a fictitious country, is in the process of making its next 5 year plan. As Minister of Health you have to prepare a Health Service Plan for the President and his Cabinet.

Curing established disease is very dependent on hospitals and on rural health centre and local dispensaries. It is not possible for Marimbia to do all that is desirable. Each decision to spend is also a decision not to spend on something else.

As Minister it is your task to decide how the funds available for Marimbia's medical needs should be allocated; centralized intensive care and elaborate equipment for the few must be balanced against primary care for many more. How will you decide?

195

The Accident

One day a serious road accident occurs at a busy intersection. Several people are injured and are taken to hospital. Three are equally badly injured and need emergency care to save their lives. There is only one doctor on duty. Witnesses to the accident have given the following information about the three people:

Mr. A – the policeman on duty at the crossing;
Mrs. B – a mother with three young children;
Mr. C – a senior student at the nearby high school.

Who should the doctor treat first?

Jane's Birthday Party

The situation: Jane's birthday party.
The people involved:

George   A smoker since he was 12 years old, who is determined to get his friends to smoke. He has a part-time job and seems to be pretty well off.

Peter   A non-smoker. He likes sport and plays football for the school and a local club. He does not like the smell of smoke and thinks it will harm his wind. He likes to be one of the group.

Maria   Not sure yet about smoking although she has smoked many times and thinks it makes her look sophisticated. She likes to go along with the group.

Jane   A non-smoker. She does not like the smell of smoke and it makes her cough. She had a heart operation when she was a baby and thinks smoking could be bad for her.

The four are together and George pulls out the cigarettes. "Come on", he says, "grow up". He offers the cigarettes round.

The Genetic Counsellor

Michael and Sophie planned to marry. In their community there was a particular genetic disease for which there was a screening test to detect the abnormal gene. Michael decided to have this test. The test showed that he was a carrier of the abnormal gene and that there was a chance that his children could suffer from the genetic disease.

Michael was very upset. He told the genetic counsellor that he was not going to tell Sophie about the test. He ordered the counsellor not to tell anyone that he was a carrier.

What should the counsellor do?

Commentary

All these examples involve scientific knowledge, and an increasing amount of technology. All in some way affect the health of the persons in the story. All require a decision to be made. But how should such decisions be made, and by whom? There is clearly no single "right" answer to any of these examples. Rather the decisions involve the values held by the people who are responsible for the decision. What are these values? What happens when people with different values are involved in making a decision?

These problems show the complexity of decisions affecting health care. They are not just medical decisions, nor scientific decisions, but they involve the social culture in which they occur. They may involve legal issues. So how are we to tackle these problems and try to arrive at the fairest decisions?

In Article 25 of the Universal Declaration of Human Rights, health is identified as a fundamental human right. In other words, societies all over the world place great value on the health, and therefore the health care, of all their citizens. Ethics has been defined (in the Oxford Dictionary) as "the study of values, rights and duties; that is, the rules by which a society lives". There are certain actions which we believe to be right, others to be wrong. This means that we should be able to explain or argue *why* we believe they are right or wrong. People individually, however, may have different views and different values, especially in a multicultural society. Moreover different ethical theories exist.

A fundamental distinction is made between theories which are based on principles determining which action should be taken, and those which consider that the outcomes of an action should be taken into account. The first kind are known as "deontological" theories, which state that people should decide what they ought to do according to predetermined rules or principles. People of a particular religious faith will follow the rules of that faith. In other words it is the action itself which is important rather than the outcome. The most common of the other major kind of ethical theories is known as "utilitarianism" in which the decision-maker judges what is best in particular circumstances by considering the consequences of an action. That action is best which brings about the greatest good for the greatest number of people. In other words, the outcomes of an action are important in deciding about a course of action. Ethical aspects of health care are those values and priorities about the health of the whole population of a society.

In 1978 the National Commission for the Protection of Human Subjects of Biomedical and Behavioural Research in the USA identified three important ethical principles (Levine, 1984). These may be applied more generally to the whole of health care. The three principles were:

Justice: the principle that equals should be treated equally.

Beneficence: the principle of doing no harm. This may be extended further to minimizing possible harms and maximizing possible benefits.

Respect for persons: the principle of autonomy. This means that individuals are capable of rational choice and are responsible for making decisions. From this flows the concept of informed consent (that is, a person must give consent to treatment which may affect his health and therefore must understand what the particular treatment involves). This raises the further concept of telling the truth to a person about his or her health status. The principle of respect also includes the concept of confidentiality or the right of a person to know.

These three basic principles may be a useful guide to begin to explore the five examples of health care given above. But how can these ideas be explored in the classroom? The rest of this section sets out some possible teaching strategies and curriculum development ideas which may be useful.

38

Challenges and Implications in Introducing Social and Ethical Issues into the Science Curriculum

V. PAYNE

Malvern Girls' College, UK

The teaching of science in its social context is demanding our attention increasingly, both nationally and internationally. However, in the first flood of enthusiasm it is easy to lose sight of our educational aims and processes. We need to be clear in our own minds about our motives for adopting this broader approach and the challenge it will present to us and our current teaching methods.

To show the human face of science and its relevance in our classroom teaching is a praiseworthy aim but, however welcome, for many science teachers this will involve a change of style from convergent methods to the more divergent methods characteristic of Arts subjects. The skills one uses as a citizen in the outside world do not necessarily transfer directly into the classroom. As science teachers we will need strategies and skills for dealing with discussion on controversial issues; as "Society teachers" we will need strategies and skills for dealing with scientific data, evidence and prediction.

For each of us there will be the need to combine the "softness" of feelings with the "hardness" of scientific knowledge. One teacher[1] favouring this broader approach has said:

"First, but not necessarily foremost, I value science and society studies for the sake of science education itself. I don't want science to be seen as the root cause of all our technological ills, nor as the panacea for all such problems, nor even just as a superbly demanding intellectual discipline. I want to show our pupils science with a human face. Secondly I value these studies for the sake of the wholeness of our children. I want them to be able not just to think well, but also to exercise personal compassion and public evaluation in the context of their science lessons. It is specifically in the balancing of

199

thought and feeling that all of us, adult and child alike, meet our greatest challenge in home, school or society at large."

Different strategies and materials are needed which can be chosen by the would-be "science/society" teacher and used flexibly to suit their own style and their pupils. Previously there has been a tendency to concentrate on the position of the pupil in the learning/teaching process. In this broader approach the position of the teacher must be considered also – it must be a comfortable one. Achieving success in introducing social issues into their science teaching provides a challenge for the science teacher.

Key Elements of Science and Society Approaches

It is possible to identify some common elements in the programmes and projects which are part of the initiative to make science more socially relevant. Using one project as an example, "Science in Society"[1] leads upper secondary level students to:

- understand the nature and limitations of scientific knowledge;
- appreciate that the use of scientific knowledge can be either beneficial or detrimental to society and the environment;
- understand the need to take account of all relevant constraints in making reasoned decisions and to develop the ability to do so;
- recognize that making decisions may involve moral considerations.

Another course, "Science in a Social Context", SISCON[2], reminds us that in the multidisciplinary approach we should include the vital "human" qualities of compassion and responsibility.

Approaches to Teaching and Learning: Simulation Games

Many of the issues, which can be included appropriately in a science/society approach do not confine themselves neatly within a science subject discipline. The approach becomes quite naturally multidisciplinary.

Involvement of the pupils is of outstanding importance – the lessons should not degenerate into the mere transmission of knowledge. Pupil involvement can be brought about through the use of decision-making simulation exercises and role-play debates. These can demonstrate the application of scientific, social and economic principles to important real-life situations whilst at the same time developing analytical, decision-making, and communication skills. Local issues are often an excellent starting point for such work.

A "game" is any contest (play) among adversaries (players) operating under constraints (rules) for an objective (winning or pay-off). A "simulation" is an operating representation of certain features of reality.

Decision-making simulation games provide a versatile and flexible medium through which a wide range of educational aims and objectives can be achieved. The advantages of such simulation games are:

- competition provides motivation for active participation;
- they provide scope for initiative and creative thought;
- they encourage the positive transfer of learning;
- they provide enjoyment and stimulation;
- they promote integration of widely related concepts into a cohesive and balanced picture;
- they help people with different subject backgrounds to work together efficiently and harmoniously.

Approaches to Teaching and Learning: Group Discussions

Several suggestions for different ways of organizing discussion have been put forward. A large class can be divided up into smaller groups of pupils and each group given a stimulus for discussion through specifically designed questions or a task to perform in a specified time. The first possibility is that the group can then report back to the whole class. In a second possibility, opinion can be distilled by organizing discussion in progressively larger groups so that finally two groups present their consensus. In this small group technique, pupils have the opportunity to speak in a less threatening atmosphere, with the stimulus of the tension of argument and of the need to come to a conclusion.

Another suggestion is for each group to record its findings/arguments on a large poster for others to comment upon. This can be particularly effective in highlighting pros and cons, written on separate posters. For example in listing the most valuable contributions, and the least, made by technology to society much discussion can centre around those elements which are common to both lists.

Further important discussion can centre on how the pupils made these value judgements.

In a recent survey of various attempts in UK to introduce social issues into their science teaching teachers expressed concern about managing discussions. It is not always possible to remain as neutral chairman and playing devil's advocate in discussion is not always a comfortable position for either teacher or pupils. We may not wish to divulge our own personal views (should we expect our pupils to do so?) or we may fear ridicule or a clash with the view of authority. One answer is for the teacher to ensure airing of all views so that the teacher's view is no more important than that of anyone else in the discussion. Clearly an atmosphere of trust is needed for discussions which involve personal feelings and views – such an atmosphere has to be created.

When organizing group discussions the teacher has two responsibilities: the selection of groups and the arrangement of the seating in the classroom. The methods of selection may vary from self-selection by the pupils to straight teacher choice. The ideal group size for discussion is between six and ten pupils. The arrangement of furniture and the seating of the group is particularly important in facilitating the flow of discussion. The obvious seating arrangement is a circle or evenly around a table, which may discourage the most dominant and may encourage the most retiring. Different groups should be as far away as possible from each other.

When the class comes together as a whole, contributions should be accepted as far as possible without direct comment to avoid feelings of approval or disapproval, which may inhibit divergent views or feelings. The teacher needs to be careful in clarifying and amplifying comments and in comparing comments from different groups, otherwise the teacher becomes the "authority". It has been suggested that the most helpful role is that of a "senior learner" who asks questions for genuine enlightenment.

References

1. "Science in Society". Heinemann and the Association for Science Education, College Lane, Hatfield, Herts AL10 9AA, UK.
2. "Science in a Social Context". The Association for Science Education, 1983.

39

A Case Study: Population as an Issue

V. PAYNE

Malvern Girls' College, UK

"Population" has been chosen as a topic to illustrate how science and society issues can be developed at upper secondary level. Two projects are reviewed to show different strategies which can be adopted or modified. Whilst these particular examples take population as a whole unit as part of their larger courses, it is possible to take parts of it in isolation. Population is a good topic to be explored by group discussion.

There can be no doubt about population as an issue of importance. With the world's population increasing by 87 million a year, there is the danger not only of food shortages but of growing discontent in the less developed countries at the industrialized countries' disproportionate share of the Earth's resources. Controlling population raises political, social, religious and educational problems: real-life practical and ethical problems for the pupils to explore.

The aim of one scheme in the UK – the Science-in-Society Project[1] – is to give pupils experience of looking at data and drawing conclusions from it so that this topic is started in a deliberately quantitative way. It provides an opportunity for the pupils to study population statistics and interpret or deduce trends from them. However, it is stressed that the amount of time spent on this activity is very much at the discretion of the teachers and their assessment of the ability and interest of their pupils. For some it may be necessary to go straight to the graphical summary for discussion. As in several other units of the course, the pupil starts with a situation close to their experience and is gradually led through a series of questions to a world view. Much time is spent in assessing the situation and going deeper than the superficial view – it is too glib to say "we must control the world's population".

The early exercises encourage the student to appreciate that it is important to consider the rate of growth of population as well as the size. Comparison is made with the growth of a biological population e.g. a

203

simple bacterial organization which reproduces by binary fission and from this emerges the idea of exponential growth and its constant doubling time. However, the point is made clearly that for world population the doubling time is decreasing – the population is increasing even more than would be given by an exponential curve. This poses difficulties in predicting with certainty the future size of the population. Population projections are made assuming that present trends continue. Many factors, expected or unexpected, may actually affect what happens. Constantly one hears the rhetorical questions: "Why don't they do something about it?" As a result of following this exercise, pupils may come to appreciate that in order to solve a problem one has to know the size of it, in particular, in this case, how rapidly the problem is changing and the uncertainty and limitation of scientific knowledge in predicting changes.

Further exercises lead to a more detailed look at how net population growth or decline depends upon the difference between the birth rate (BR) and the death rate (DR). For a particular country the growth rate (GR) is given by GR = BR − DR + M where M = net migration into the country. Discussion can centre around the way in which developed and less developed countries differ.

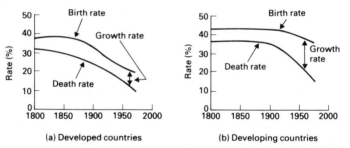

(a) Developed countries   (b) Developing countries

On a worldwide scale, as a result of new health technology, and the ensuing dramatic increase in life expectancy the death rate is now less than half the birth rate, which has declined little.

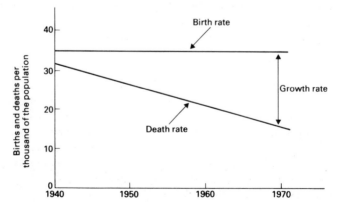

The diagram below from the International Labour Organization indicated the population in 1970 (shaded part) and the full length gives the anticipated total at the end of the century. Whether dealing with statistics or assessing graphical material, the pupil is urged to make comparisons and to consider implications. Gradually the shape of a population policy is beginning to emerge.

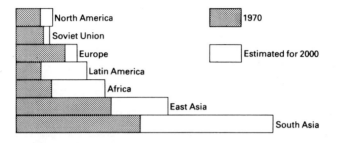

A second comparison is made with a biological population growing in a finite area and the eventual flattening out of the population as it reaches an equilibrium state. "Why does this flattening occur?" "Could the same thing happen with human populations?"

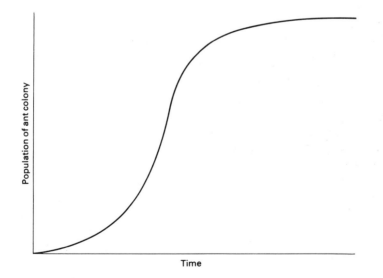

There is another factor which must be taken into consideration, namely, the age structure of the population. The two schemes converge here in making a comparison of the population pyramids for a country with a very rapidly expanding population (B) and for a more stable population with a slow expansion rate (A).

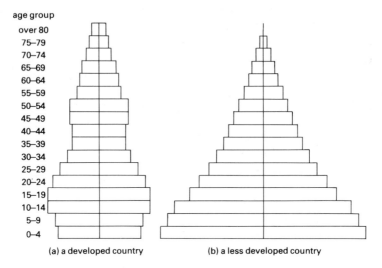

age group

over 80	
75–79	
70–74	
65–69	
60–64	
55–59	
50–54	
45–49	
40–44	
35–39	
30–34	
25–29	
20–24	
15–19	
10–14	
5–9	
0–4	

(a) a developed country   (b) a less developed country

In (B) there is a very high proportion of the population in the reproductive category and the very broad base implies an even larger percentage of young people ready to move into the reproductive category over the next 15 years. This population structure is the position in a very high proportion of less developed countries so that even if better medical care is accompanied by a vigorous campaign of family planning, their populations must continue to expand for at least 30 years.

Attitudes towards birth control will not necessarily be the same in developed and less developed countries. In one country alone there will be different communities with differing views and this will be reflected within the school. It may not be easy for a pupil hearing the injunctions of family or religion, to defend a point of view or course of action, which perhaps they do not understand or believe at this age. Contraception is a delicate personal issue and at this point it is particularly important that the science teachers assess their confidence in dealing with discussion about it. The Science-in-Society Project[1] provides background reading material and suggests that a doctor or nurse might be called in to lead the discussion. On the other hand, contraception may already be dealt with in another part of the curriculum, e.g. health education, "personal relationships" or "life skills" courses.

In another route, the class might address itself to the questions "How far can politicians or scientists go in determining population control, since it could be argued that it is a fundamental liberty for man and woman to decide how many children they have?", "Is it possible to legislate over birth control?". Without legislation we must rely on the climate of opinion.

"Is it possible to control population by indirect means of coaxing and encouragement?", "Who should be responsible for planning population control – scientists, or politicians, or both?". In formulating policy, politicians should consult scientific demographers; scientists should be able to provide effective methods of contraception, which are acceptable and appropriate.

SISCON[2] develops further this theme of what is acceptable and appropriate within different cultures in its attempt to minimize the remote attitude that can be taken towards health in the Less Developed Countries, reminding pupils that Western science and technology does not transplant readily into other societies. Applying Western style family planning in another country may be seen as interference in its internal affairs.

Pupils are invited to consider other factors, besides religious beliefs, against programmes for planning family size in the LDCs. These include: the desirability of an expanding population producing more man-power and stimulating the economy; medically supervised birth control is too expensive; families may need children to help provide income for the family; sons are needed to care for parents in old age; expectation of a high level of infant mortality leads to a general tendency towards large families to allow for inevitable loss.

Governments in favour of a family planning programme see in this the only possible method of decreasing unemployment, raising standards of health and education, preserving the fertility of the land and stimulating savings.

Confidence in the survival of children, the visible chances of good education and a better job are positive influences.

In conclusion then, the topic of "population" illustrates well the tension and delicate balance between the beneficial effects and the detrimental effects of the application of scientific knowledge. Discussion might conclude with considering this quotation.[1]

"The dilemma is this. All the impulses of decent humanity, all the dictates of religion and all the traditions of medicine insist that suffering should be relieved, curable diseases cured, preventable diseases prevented. The obligation is regarded as unconditional: it is not permitted to argue that the suffering is due to folly, that the children are not wanted, that the patient's family would be happier if he died. All that may be so; but to accept it as a guide to action would lead to a degradation of standards of humanity by which civilization would be permanently and indefinitely poorer.

"Some might take the purely biological view that if men will breed like rabbits they must be allowed to die like rabbits. Most people would still say no. But suppose it were certain now that the pressure of increasing population, uncontrolled by disease, would lead not only to widespread exhaustion of the soil and of other capital resources but also to continuing and increasing international tension and disorder, making it hard for civilization to survive: would the majority of humane and reasonable people then change their minds?

"If ethical principles deny our right to do evil in order that good may come, are we justified in doing good when the foreseeable consequence is evil?"

References

1. Science-in-Society Project. Association for Science Education, College Lane, Hatfield, Hertfordshire AL10 9AA, UK.
2. Science in a Social Context. Association for Science Education.

40

An Example of a Decision-making Simulation Game "The Marimbian Health Service Project"

J. L. LEWIS
Malvern College, UK

When the Science-in-Society Project was developed in the UK by the Association for Science Education, it was agreed to include a section on "Health and Medicine". A survey had shown that children in secondary schools were much more interested in disease than in health (as others have found to be the case in certain developed countries). It was accepted that there was a need for students to think more positively about health; to appreciate the importance of prevention rather than cure; to consider wider issues than themselves. Promoting awareness of health problems in developing countries became an important part of the course. One of the Science-in-Society Readers, for example, contrasted malaria and small-pox: smallpox has been virtually eradicated by a massive international exercise whereas there is more malaria in the world in the 1980s than there was in the 1960s.

Perhaps the most telling statistic is "the paradox of the quarters" as illustrated below:

(a) Three-quarters of the population in developing countries is rural, only one-quarter is urban.

(b) Yet three-quarters of the health care is urban directed, only one-quarter is directed at the rural population.

(c) Three-quarters of the diseases that affect people in developing countries are preventable, only one-quarter need care.

(d) Yet three-quarters of the health budget is spent on attempts at cure, the massive task of prevention has to be content with a mere one-quarter.

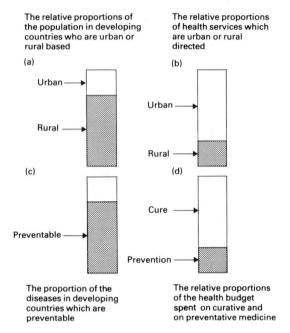

The relative proportions of the population in developing countries who are urban or rural based

The relative proportions of health services which are urban or rural directed

The proportion of the diseases in developing countries which are preventable

The relative proportions of the health budget spent on curative and on preventative medicine

Once again, it is not adequate merely to point out these facts to young people. It is educationally desirable to get them involved by getting them to *do* something. It was for this reason that the Science-in-Society Project developed its decision-making exercise, the Marimbian Health Service Project.

The Marimbian Health Service Project

The project takes the form of a study of the health needs of Marimbia, a fictitious African country, and of how those needs might be met with the resources available.

The aims of the project are:

(a) To enable students, who have grown up in the expectation that effective medical help is always readily accessible, to increase their understanding of the health problems of developing countries, and particularly of rural areas.

(b) To help them to perceive that lack of resources compels a choice between prevention, cure and care of the incurable; that helping some means leaving others without aid.

(c) To emphasize that a health service does not arise from expressions of sympathy with the suffering or from vague benevolence, however sincere. Health service planners can fight disease only by making effective use of a limited amount of the wealth which others have created.

(d) To provide experience of the problems of an imaginary country which may lead students to a greater awareness of the advantages which they enjoy in their own and which they take too easily for granted.

Each student should have a copy of the student booklet, and in addition there is a separate guide for the teacher, which includes suggested answers to the questions asked in the student booklet. Not that there are necessarily right or wrong answers, but it gives encouragement to teachers, who are perhaps dealing with topics outside their knowledge and experience, to have some indication of possible answers and points which may be raised in discussion.

The student booklet gives first a guide to the geography and economy of Marimbia, with an outline of the present health service arrangements. It is necessary to know about the size of the country, the distribution of the population and details of the road systems and of communication in the country. Economic aspects of the country are important, as it is also important that the costs of training doctors, nurses and medical auxiliaries are appreciated in order that decisions can be made. (The national currency in Marimbia is taken as the fictional Ella, abbreviated to E, rather than using the dollar, so that the exercise can continue to be used as the years go by unaffected by inflation!)

The booklet contains a series of tasks (labelled A–G) interspersed with additional information. Students are expected to work through tasks A–F singly or in pairs; the questions involved can be answered using common sense and the information given about Marimbia.

When the six tasks have been completed, the students assume in task G the role of the Minister of Health or his advisers and prepare a report for the President and his Cabinet. This report should give an outline of the Health Service Plan for the next 5 years.

As explained in the separate Teacher's Guide, it is not possible for Marimbia to do all that is desirable. There is no perfect solution or "right" answer, and this can be emphasized by pointing out that each decision to spend is also a decision not to spend on something else.

The following are topics which are likely to be discussed in detail:

What are the chief causes of sickness and death in Marimbia?

Do these point more to the need for curative or for preventive medicine?

What are the social and economic conditions of Marimbian life which will affect the planning of the health service?

What is the catchment area for a hospital? What are the transport problems for Marimbians wishing to make use of its services?

Is it better to build large Regional hospitals, smaller District hospitals or many more Rural Health Centres?

Should the policy be to train more doctors or many more medical assistants? What factors influence this decision?

What proportion of limited national resources should be expended on the care of the elderly and of incurables?

Of course many of these issues, particularly the last one, raise all sorts of ethical problems, all of which are worthy of discussion and help to promote awareness of the wider issues involved.

Benefits to be Gained from the Project

One of the benefits of working through the Marimbian Health Service Project in an English school is that it inevitably forces comparisons with our own health service. For this reason the following postscript appears at the end of the student's booklet.

> "You have now studied the Health Service of this fictitious country Marimbia. This should have shown you some of the problems with which a developing country has to contend and the kind of decisions which its policy makers must necessarily make. As a postscript you may like to think about some of the problems of the health service in your own country – and the decisions which have to be made concerning it. Many of these are similar to those which had to be made for Marimbia.

> "In both countries you can provide only what the country can afford – as the service has to be financed from the funds available. In both countries it is necessary to decide what proportions of the limited resources should be devoted to cure, to prevention and to care."

The postscript then continues by asking fundamental questions about the British Health Service. Is it really a National Disease Service? Is enough positive action being taken to encourage Health? Have we been too unsuccessful in persuading people to eat less, drink less, stop smoking and stop sitting around instead of taking exercise in outdoor activities? How might matters be improved?

Role-playing Exercises

The Marimbian Health Service Project is not the only decision-making exercise in the Health section of the Science-in-Society course. There is also the Dental Health Project, which is based on the hypothesis that a Health Authority has recommended fluoridation, that is, adding fluoride to the water supply in order to reduce dental decay. This role-playing exercise takes the form of a simulated meeting of a local authority, at which a final decision has to be made. There is a set of role cards, half of which contain arguments in favour of fluoridation and half arguments against. As explained in the Teacher's Guide, these cards are distributed in advance of the "meeting" so that students can prepare their case. Once all the students have put their case, there can be a general discussion and a free vote is taken. This is obviously a totally different type of exercise, but it has proved popular as a teaching technique. It has the advantage that it also promotes communication skills: students have the opportunity to prepare, present and defend a case from a given point of view in which scientific aspects can be considered to whatever depth is commensurate with their ability. The success of the Science-in-Society decision-making exercises is beyond doubt: many pupils describe them as the best part of the course.

41

An Issue Approach to Teaching and Learning in Secondary School Biology

M. BRUMBY
Monash University, Australia

In the last 10 years or so there have been quite spectacular developments in many areas of biological science. Medical scientists in different parts of the world have many times succeeded in fertilizing a human ovum with human sperms *in vitro* (that is, in the laboratory) and successfully implanting this fertilized egg into a woman who could not conceive a child naturally. We can detect certain genetic defects in the developing foetus as early as 6 weeks' gestation. Babies born after only 24 weeks may successfully survive. We can transplant many different organs and tissues from one person to another. Artificial organs are being developed; doctors "look at" internal organs using new technology; agricultural scientists genetically engineer new varieties of crops which are resistant to disease – these are just a few examples of quite amazing developments in biological science.

However, it is probably true to say that none of the scientific technologies themselves, nor even the scientific knowledge on which the technologies were based, are in the core biology curriculum of the great majority of secondary schools.

Should such developments, and their possible consequences, be included in senior school biology curricula? How much biological knowledge does one need to know in order to be able to understand the significance of new developments and the nature of the controversies and of the interest shown by the ordinary people and by the media? One of the central aims of education is to help prepare students for the world in which they will live. Their lives will increasingly be shaped by science. Decisions will have to be taken about the application of rapid new scientific developments. But who should make these decisions and on what basis?

As McConnell said as early as 1928: "The problems associated with technological development may primarily not be problems of technology.

Rather they may be problems among us and between us, problems in large measure the result of a pluralist society in which common purpose, common value and common images (of the future) are no longer present . . . They are issues involving conflicts between values and goals among persons . . ."

Should schools in general and science education in particular even discuss values? If it is accepted by individual teachers that discussions of the consequences of new technologies *should* be part of the relevant science curriculum, then they may need encouragement to introduce different teaching and learning strategies. One such curriculum development has occurred in science secondary biology in Victoria, Australia, with the introduction of an optimal programme of study called Issues in Biology (Brumby, 1984). Let us outline the important features of an "issue" approach with the example of organ transplantation.

Organ Transplantation as an Issue

Organ transplantation (for example the heart or kidney) raises many issues. One is when may an organ be removed from the body of a person who has, for example, been injured in a road accident. Should life-supporting technology be continued in order to keep the organs in a good condition? This raises the question of defining when a person can legally be described as dead, for one cannot remove such organs until after death.

In 1982 the parliament of Victoria, Australia, enacted the Human Tissue Act. One of its clauses contained, for the first time, a *legal* (that is, not just medical) definition of death. The Act states:

Part IX – Definition of Death
S.41. For the purpose of the law of Victoria, a person has died when there has occurred –
(a) irreversible cessation of circulation of blood in the body of the person; or
(b) irreversible cessation of all function of the brain of the person.

What biological concepts are contained in this statement? There are two. One is about blood circulation and the second is about brain function. In other words the law-makers have used scientific concepts in drafting this legal definition. But is this use sufficiently precise from a scientific perspective?

This definition does not make two things clear. First, how the two signs are to be observed. Section 41(a) implies the presence or absence of a beating heart, perhaps as shown by an electrocardiogram (ECG). Section 41(b) may be detected by the presence or absence of any electrical activity in the brain, as shown by an electroencephalogram (EEG). Secondly, whether the two signs (blood circulation and brain function) must be occurring naturally, unaided by machines. Artificial life-support machines can maintain both blood circulation and breathing. Such technology therefore already creates problems, for example

- If a person is not able to carry out these two functions unaided, are they already dead and the machines attached to a corpse?
- If the person is still considered "alive" while on the machines, then does switching off the machines constitute killing the person?

Elsewhere in the Act there are clauses which set out who should give consent to removal of organs, what age-limits should be used, and a prohibition of the sale of organs (for example, a single kidney). But a legal answer to a problem created by new biomedical technology may not be completely adequate. Let us return to the second part of this clause.

Section 41(b) (often referred to as the "brain-death" clause) is a new criterion for deciding whether a person has died. The phrase "all function" suggests activity of the brain stem (where body temperature, blood pressure and breathing are controlled) as well as the brain cerebral cortex (where consciousness, memory, thinking, feelings, and responses to the environment are carried out) must both have stopped. A person in a deep coma, as a result of permanent damage to the cortex, is, under this definition, still clearly alive. This analysis shows the problem created by sophisticated life-support technology and the need by our society to re-examine what it is to be "alive". Is it just to be a member of the species *Homo sapiens*, or do we include in our standard biological definitions characteristics which suggest a *conscious* person who can think, solve problems and interact with his/her environment?

All around the world societies place the greatest value and respect for human life. This is clearly expressed in the Universal Declaration of Human Rights. Article 1 states: "All human beings are born free and equal in dignity and rights. They are endowed with reason and conscience and should act towards one another in a spirit of brotherhood." Article 3 states: "Everyone has the right to life, liberty and security of person."

But even statements such as these may not help decide, for example, *who* should receive a scarce kidney transplant when the number of donors is much less than the number of people requiring a new organ. So ethical and social issues arise in addition to the legal questions set out in the law designed to regulate this new technology.

This example of organ transplantation is a brief introduction to an "issue" approach in biology. The aims of an issue approach are much wider than simply as a means of increasing students' knowledge about a particular biological development. The primary focus is not on knowledge but on the skills of analysis, assimilation, evaluation and decision-making about the application of science to society. However, these skills, and others such as asking questions, objectivity, interpretation vs. observation, unbiased reasoning, are all essential components of "scientific thinking". This does not mean that the relevant biological knowledge is not important, for it is essential background to understanding an issue. What is more important, however, is that decisions have to be made about what *is* relevant knowledge to an issue. By taking an issue approach, students are encouraged to think critically about the issue and seek out relevant biological knowledge.

An issue approach clearly involves a multidisciplinary study, particularly examining the boundaries between science and the legal and philosophical foundations of society. Such studies should vividly reveal the very great impact science has had, and continues to have, on the world in which we live.

It is clear that biology and science teachers may need to broaden their own expertise in order to be resource people about relevant laws, human rights and ethical principles. This is the challenge of teaching in this way. In providing some experience of how to seek out relevant knowledge, to evaluate developments critically and to contribute to informed decisions, not only may we begin to prepare our students for the increasingly technological world in which they will live, but we will achieve much for ourselves as learners as well as teachers.

The formal syllabus in HSC Biology sets out a brief guide of what is expected of the student in this optional Study, using an issue approach.

Topic 10: Issues in Biology

Each student is to make an analytical study of at least one social issue which involves biological knowledge being applied to an aspect of human life, and over which there is significant community controversy. Some examples follow.

* Producing human infants by *in vitro* fertilization
* Using genetic counselling in advising prospective parents
* Birth control to limit human population
* Producing new species and varieties by recombinant-DNA technology
* The effects of smoking, alcohol or drugs of addiction
* The use of laboratory animals in scientific research

For the issue chosen, the student is to

* identify the critical questions over which there is disagreement
* find out – as completely as possible – the arguments used on both sides of the issues, using library references and other published information
* participate in thorough reasoned debate with other students
* present a written report which sets out the issues clearly, thoroughly and concisely

---

Assessing Students' Written Projects

Rather than formal tests or exams which focus on knowledge, a written report allows for the objectives of an "issues" approach to be evaluated.

Since the objectives focus on exploration of the issue rather than finding an answer to the issue, skills of information gathering, analysis, and evaluation should be reflected in the overall assessment. Students need to understand these criteria of assessment and may be involved in the relative weighting of marks. They also need to know that they do not have to come to "a conclusion" (that is, give the "right" answer) as a result of their project.

The following points may act as a useful guide to assessing a written report:

(a) a clear definition of the issue(s) to be studied;

(b) identification of the critical questions over which there is debate;

(c) analysis of these questions, including scientific, legal, ethical and social aspects;

(d) objective evaluation and balanced reporting on both sides of the debate;

(e) identification and consideration of the authority of information sources;

(f) thoroughness of the initial planning of the study and effort put into both the actual study and writing it up (for example, details of literature search);

(g) summing up, or concluding section which shows both the degree of insight gained from the study, and whether the report is internally consistent with item (a) above.

Selection of Issues

Wherever possible, students should be encouraged to select their own issue. Availability of resources may be a constraining factor which planning in advance may resolve.

In early meetings some teachers were concerned that the "gee-whiz" high profile issues such as IVF may be disproportionally selected. Ideas for possible projects, associated resources and reading lists were included in the Option book (Brumby, 1984) commissioned by the Australian Science Teacher Association as part of the series "Topics in Biology". An important step in developing students' ideas is to help them move from a general *topic* area on to identify the actual issue(s) involved. "What are some of the issues/questions?" is a key question to pose. Many students, for example, can identify an area of interest (such as "heart transplantation") but need to be helped to identify relevant *issues*. Newspaper articles can be helpful at this early stage. Clarity in identifying them is helpful in actually getting started in a project, particularly if time is restricted.

Class-based Activities

There is a variety of class-based activities which focus on the issues while students may be researching their project. Class size is a pragmatic factor influencing the scope of activities. It may be possible to have one major conceptual theme which provides a core biological knowledge component and which allows several related individual small group projects. Human reproduction and human fertility is an example of such a theme. The introductory lessons can cover the scientific core (which may include laboratory work) while students begin collecting information relevant to their chosen issue.

Other student-based activities could be to find out what others think about the issue being investigated. The design of unbiased questionnaires, surveys within a school or within a local community, and analysis of simple demographic variables (such as age and sex of participants) is a worthwhile experience. Communication skills, from interviewing strangers (such as a lawyer, a local member of Parliament) and consideration of how to respect the privacy of others, may all be developed. Various audio-visual programmes or guest speakers can be used to trigger discussion of different perspectives. A literature search, or reading of selected scientific papers, or the student's writing a report based on a scientific paper for a general audience are other possibilities. An excellent activity can be to review critically a series of newspaper articles (Are the headlines an accurate reflection of the article? Does a particular paper present only one view?), and to report to the class. Restating a particular law in everyday language may be a good task. A future time-perspective (set the scene in 50 years' time and "look back" on the present issue) may result in interesting ideas. Class debates may be organized with one group of students researching the two major sides of the issue. Skills of questioning, information gathering, evaluation of data, objectivity and the difficulty of making decisions in the light of incomplete knowledge, and written and oral communication skills are all therefore developed during class time.

Another strategy is to have small groups taking on the roles of various characters. For example, in the case of the genetic counselling issue mentioned on page 196, three groups can be formed, assigned to Michael, Sophie and the genetic counsellor, respectively. Each group can focus on the goals and rights of each character and their duties to themselves, to

	goals	rights	duties
Michael			
Sophie			
Counsellor			

each of the other characters and to society in general. Each group can then present to the whole class how they see these goals, rights and duties. The teacher may draw up a table on the blackboard during the presentation. Students should identify the conflicts between individuals and the community, and pose the question about whose interests are being served by such a screening programme. In such a group role-play, an individual student's views are not revealed, rather a "group view" is presented. Identification of goals, rights and duties leads on to identifying the steps in decision-making.

In all work on ethical decision-making the need for respect of others' ideas is of the greatest importance. Competing views are bound to be expressed. It is important that students do not criticize *each other*, but focus on the *view*. For example it is permissible to say: "I do not agree with that view because . . .", but not to say: "You're crazy saying that!"

Another good example is the cigarette-smoking issue (see page 196). The teacher may ask:

1. What the topic is . . . . (the influence of peers on smoking)
2. What Jane's goal is . . . . (to look after her own health)
3. The constraints . . . . (wanting to be part of the group, etc)
4. The alternative courses . . . . (to accept or not to accept the cigarette)
5. Evaluation of the alternatives (this may be as a risk or costs vs. benefits analysis)

And then it may be left to the students to come to their own decisions. In other words the teacher's role has been to help guide the students through how decisions can be logically and ethically made, but not to instruct them "You should not smoke, it is bad for your health".

Professional Development of Teachers

In-service training sessions are crucial to give an opportunity for teachers to consider different teaching strategies, and discuss any questions they have.

One question discussed at some length with teachers concerning free student choice of their project was the degree of personal involvement in a sensitive topic. Should a student be encouraged to study the issue of euthanasia, for example, if it is known that the student's parent or grandparent has terminal cancer? There is obviously no clear answer to this question. Overall, teachers were of the opinion that if a student expressed an interest in a topic then this should wherever possible be encouraged, with sensitivity to students' personal growth.

Although a primary aim is to encourage respect for different views and values, certain issues require particular sensitivity. For example one teacher suggested inviting a physically disabled student from another class to come and talk to the class. If the issue under study was problems about the birth of severely disabled or extremely premature babies, then it would take very great skill to ensure that the value of that individual disabled student's life was *not* being critically evaluated by his or her peers. It would be completely unacceptable to place a burden on any student, so those issues with a life-and-death component should be chosen, with restraint, by mature students. No students should be obliged to study issues which for personal reasons they do not wish to study.

In these science/society approaches, it is the task of the teacher to create a framework within which students can explore safely their ideas and views. However, in some of the teaching strategies, particularly role-play, it is all too easy for the student to become immersed in the role-playing itself. They lose sight of the final end-point, which is consideration of one's own views and those of others in formulating a final viewpoint.

It is tempting for the teacher to summarize by drawing together some consensus – but this will be the consensus perceived by the teacher, not by the students. If the aim of the exercise is to reach a consensus, this should be done by the students through a dynamic group exercise. On the other hand, it is essential that students emerge from a particular activity less confused than when they started. Thus a short debriefing session may be necessary for individual students to clarify their position.

Some topics may upset certain students because of personal circumstances or arouse feelings which they may not then know how to deal with. Teachers may need to make a time allowance for this at the end of an activity. In this time students can make comments in private, which may be necessary for them to resolve some personal feelings about the situation.

Confidentiality and Privacy

Class activities may result in a student seeking the advice of a teacher concerning a personal decision about a health topic. This may occur outside lesson time. A teacher's role may be difficult here, for the majority of secondary students are under the legal age of maturity and so are under parental responsibility. The dilemma for teachers is whether she/he should consider all such information in confidence, or whether they should inform the parents (or school principal). A very high priority is placed on confidentiality in the professional teacher–student relationship. However, this should not be given in an unqualified way.

The teacher is best advised to listen to the student's problem and try and help the student come to his or her own decision about the best course of action (for example whether to tell parents about the problem). The most difficult area is perhaps in sex education and human relationships.

Another question is raised by the use of a survey data collection which may be identified to a particular student. For example: "A common homework activity in a drug education programme is to survey; make a list of all the drugs you find in your home!" It is possible that students discover knowledge about other family members which they did not know. This in itself raises questions of privacy. In addition, the possible reactions of other class members may be embarrassing to a particular student. As a general guide, any survey data collection should be anonymous, and the teachers themselves may need to collect and collate any questionnaire information.

Reference

Brumby (1984) *Issues in Biology*. Topics in Biology series, published in association with Science Teachers Association of Victoria. Thomas Nelson Australia.

PART VII

*Diseases of
Global Importance*

Introduction

This section opens with a brief contribution on what might be taught at what level concerning diseases of global importance, and is followed by a more detailed paper on the classification of diseases and how use can be made of classification in the classroom.

This is followed by contributions on cancer as a topic in health education, on bilharzia, on carcinogenicity induced by environmental agents, such as aflatoxins. One case study, namely malaria, is treated in some depth and its place in science programmes is reviewed and discussed.

The paper on leprosy is important as leprosy is a disease with a special social stigma and it advocates that the level of professionalism be raised by enhancing and co-ordinating the skills of the different professional groups such as medical students, physicians, clinical specialists and research workers.

The final contribution gives an example of how a particular category of disease, namely roundworm infections, could be introduced into school science.

42

What Might Be Taught about Diseases

G. R. MEYER

Macquarie University, Australia

There are many diseases of global importance and it would not be possible to consider them all in a school science syllabus or even within a general community health education programme. Further, there are different priorities from country to country and region to region. In countries such as Australia, UK and Western Germany the most significant diseases in some order of priority, are cardiovascular diseases, cancer, allergic diseases, psychoses and other forms of mental illness, together with infectious diseases, mainly viral in nature. In tropical Asian countries, such as India and Thailand, acute gastro-intestinal disease, parasitic worm infections, malaria, influenza and conjunctivitis are the central problems. In Southern tropical Africa, for example in Zambia, the main diseases are malaria, the diseases of malnutrition such as kwashiorkor and marasmus, sexually-transmitted diseases, and worm infestations such as bilharzia.

It is suggested, therefore, that at least for health education at school level, three approaches be adopted. Firstly, in the primary school the main diseases of local significance be dealt with, with special stress on prevention and control. Secondly, in the secondary school, several case studies of relevant local diseases be treated in some depth, probably in the general science or biology course. In particular, special attention should be given to those aspects which could be effectively demonstrated by meaningful practical work in the laboratory, for example, malaria and parasitic worm infections. Thirdly, in the secondary school, a general overview be given of diseases of global importance, treated from the point of view of the various ways in which such diseases could be grouped or classified and how they could be controlled and perhaps eventually eradicated.

At higher levels of education, including teacher education and the training of health specialists, in-depth studies of specific diseases would of course be essential.

It is recommended that when dealing with this aspect of health, teachers sound a positive note showing how advances in technology are increasingly controlling and even in some cases totally eliminating some diseases. The techniques of biotechnology could be especially emphasized as providing a powerful tool for the potential eradication of certain types of disease worldwide.

43

Classification of Diseases

G. R. MEYER
Macquarie University, Australia

It is important to give school students some understanding of diseases prevailing in different areas of the world. One approach could be to consider how diseases might be classified or grouped, and there are several ways of grouping. This is an especially suitable way of treating this topic in secondary schools.

Suggested systems of classifying diseases are outlined below. These are not intended to be prescriptive and one interesting exercise might be to challenge students to suggest alternatives. This focuses attention on the concept of classification as an important process in science.

The Medical Profession's Classification

The medical profession's system of disease classification is classically divided into those that you are born with ("congenital") and those that you acquire during life ("acquired"). Congenital diseases include diseases of development such as birth defects and genetic diseases (for example, sickle cell anaemia). Congenital diseases may or may not be treatable, but they are rarely curable, at least at present. Acquired diseases include infections (those caused by bacteria, viruses etc), infestations (roundworms, tape-worms), diseases due to poor nutrition (kwashiorkor), cancer, and diseases of the body systems (heart, brain etc) including hormonal defects.

An obvious approach for differentiating these concepts could be through the genetic strand of secondary school biology. Acquired diseases can be dealt with through studies of diversity and adaptation. At primary school level the case study approach is recommended with a stress on causes and on how society should cope with congenital disease and control contagious disease. Visual aids are especially useful in this area. Whenever possible and ethically appropriate, practical investigations should be undertaken such as community surveys and laboratory observations, particularly in the higher grades of the secondary school.

One final point should be stressed: an understanding of the medical

231

profession's system of classification of diseases must rest on a good knowledge and understanding of the structure and functions of the human body which can best be conveyed through the school science curriculum.

Economic Loss (Mortality) and Economic Burden (Morbidity)

Some diseases cause death, while others cause permanent deformity or debility. Mortality (death) is an acute problem, but severe disability puts an economic and social burden on the community. Epidemics (typhoid, cholera, plague) may cause massive loss of life. Loss of wage-earners and workers will have economic consequences.

Morbidity (debility), that is, a low physiological state, results from diseases which do not necessarily cause death, but lower the general well-being of the body (malaria, common cold, bilharzia). Examples of diseases that may produce long-lasting disabilities are leprosy, river blindness and mental illness.

This type of classification will be considered in courses in social studies, economics and civics, but science teachers should also consider these important economic and human aspects of disease.

Prevention versus Cure

Infectious diseases either respond to treatment with appropriate antibiotic chemotherapy or resolve themselves. Many forms of cancer respond to treatment by chemotherapy or radiotherapy. Nutritional diseases may be cured by correct nutrition. Some diseases, however, are at present incurable: examples are some viral infections (AIDS), metabolic and genetic diseases and some forms of mental illness. In the future, of course, scientists may find cures for such diseases. However, prevention is better than cure.

Prevention of diseases includes immunization, attention to hygiene and sanitation, avoidance of contact in the case of infectious disease, eradication of vectors (mosquitoes carrying malaria) and having a balanced diet. Nations have to balance the cost of massive prevention programmes against the social and economic cost of ill health.

This type of classification highlights the importance of attitudes and values. Students should appreciate their personal responsibilities in maintaining good health. They should also appreciate the roles of government agencies, community programmes and international bodies, such as WHO. An especially important aspect of this approach is the opportunity it provides to stress in science courses the role of new scientific technologies in the control and treatment of disease.

Geographical Distribution

Although many diseases show a geographical distribution, this often results from economic and cultural factors rather than from climatic, geological or ecological factors. It is a fact that individuals in developing countries have a different spectrum of diseases (more infections and a consequently lower life expectancy) compared with those in developed nations who survive only to succumb finally to cancer, heart disease etc. However, if the developing nations had access to the economic resources of the advanced countries this could all change.

One only has to look at urban/rural gradients to see the effect of the economic environments. In some countries, in the town there is access to medical and preventive treatment and higher wages allow better nutrition, etc, in contrast to the situation in remote villages. Some nations in tropical areas (for example, Hong Kong and Singapore) have very good medical and nutritional standards because they are economically successful.

This geographical approach to classification is flexible and open to different interpretations. However, it provides an opportunity to show that social and economic conditions differ from region to region throughout the world and that diseases play an important role in determining these socio-economic parameters and vice versa. It also demonstrates that appropriate programmes of intervention can seriously affect socio-economic standards.

Age

Certain diseases are much more common at certain ages. At the extremes there are diseases connected with birth (for example, rhesus incompatibility) and those of old age (cancer, arthritis, rheumatism, cataract and arterio-sclerosis). If a person's life expectancy is short then he or she may not survive to experience the diseases of the elderly. Here again we can see the division between developed and developing nations.

Anyone can succumb to infectious diseases, but in practice the older a person is, the more likely it is that he or she has his or her own protection, either acquired or by immunization. So infectious diseases are most usually encountered in the young.

Poor nutrition can affect everyone, but it is more damaging in the growing child.

This approach is useful to show the incidence of diseases according to age, but does not imply that certain diseases are totally restricted to specific age groups. It is also useful to approach the topic of disease by using available demographic data and could be introduced not only through biology, but also through the social sciences. This approach also implies that different intervention programmes would be suitable for different age groups.

44

Cancer as a Topic in Health Education

S. CHAWLA and P. PANAG

Cancer is the uncontrolled growth of certain cells of the body which in later stages may spread to other parts of the body. Its very name incites dread and a feeling of doom in the public mind.

It is not widely enough known that, with early diagnosis, prompt treatment and subsequent regular medical check-ups, many forms of cancer can be cured or kept under control for long periods. It is this optimistic approach to cancer which needs emphasis.

There are certain factors which can be avoided without too great a difficulty, thereby reducing the risk of cancer:

- hot spicy foods may increase the risk of stomach cancer;

- smoking increases the chances of a person developing lung cancer;

- repeated injury and infection of the birth canal (cervix) which may happen when a large number of children are born to a woman, increases the risk of cancer of the cervix;

- chewing the betel nut and/or tobacco and irritation by ill-fitting dentures predispose to development of cancer of the cheek lining and mouth;

- single exposure to large doses of radiation, for example, by nuclear explosions or leakage from nuclear plants, as well as repeated exposure to small doses of radiation whether employed for diagnostic purposes or for treating cancer, can itself lead to development of cancer;

- excessive exposure to ultraviolet rays of the sun increases the risk of skin cancer;

- certain chemical agents such as aniline dyes are often associated with increased occurrence of cancer;

- industries where radioactive substances and asbestos are used predispose the workers to the development of cancer unless stringent precautions are taken;
- exhaust fumes and environmental pollution have also been implicated.

A significant aspect of cancer prevention and cancer control is to appreciate that not all cancers are alike. The cancer group of diseases includes some varieties which are readily accessible and therefore can be diagnosed and treated early (cancer of the breast, mouth and cervix). Some others are deep seated, and by the time they give rise to symptoms it may be too late to cure them (cancer of the stomach, or lungs for example). Certain types of cancer grow very slowly and appropriate treatment can eliminate them or at least keep them under control for long periods. There are others which spread very fast and are difficult to control. Even in the same type of cancer, that is cancer involving the same site, different patients respond differently to the same treatment, as many factors determine the outcome of treatment. However, early diagnosis is important in all types of cancer.

There are certain warning signals which may indicate cancer. It is very important to stress, however, that these signs may not always indicate the presence of cancer.

- lump or nodule in the breast or blood discharge from the nipple;
- sudden change in the size and colour of a wart or a mole;
- unexplainable change in bowel habits;
- difficulty in swallowing;
- excessive blood loss during the menstrual period or bleeding at times of sexual intercourse;
- white patches or swelling in cheek lining or tongue;
- a lump anywhere in the body;
- localized swelling of part of an arm or leg, without injury;
- unexplained fever and weight loss;
- passing of blood in urine or stools;
- persistent cough.

The most important task of health education is to eliminate the intense feeling of fear and helplessness associated with this disease. It should be emphasized to the public through health education that some cancers can be diagnosed early and completely cured; in most others life can be prolonged and made comfortable.

Correct information about cancer is extremely important. The widely held belief that cancer is incurable and always causes intractable pain has to be rectified. The emphasis should be that early diagnosis and appropriate treatment can cure cancer. This aim can be achieved by exposure to the experiences of real-life patients who have been cured as part of the curriculum content.

45

Bilharzia

M. S. SELIM
Cairo, Egypt

Bilharzia is one of the most serious diseases in Africa. The parasite causes great suffering, it affects the liver, kidneys and bladder. The debility caused by it results in lack of productivity, and the great economic loss to Egypt alone is estimated in millions of working days. A large percentage of children of school age suffer from it, especially in rural areas, where children are always in contact with infected water in the slow-moving irrigation canals.

Infection is by a tiny microscopic organism, cercaria, swimming in the water, which penetrates the skin of people in the water. It moves through the circulatory system, undergoing many changes until it settles in the liver system. The male and female live attached. Eggs are produced and they penetrate the urinary bladder wall causing bleeding on urination. When disposed in water after urination, the eggs hatch into a miracidium (larva) which swims about until it encounters and enters the body of another host, a small snail. After some time great numbers of cercaria come out of the snail and penetrate the human skin to complete the life cycle.

To combat bilharzia, its life cycle must be broken by not allowing the eggs to reach canal waters by not urinating in them. The cycle can also be broken by destroying the snails by mechanical or chemical means. Patients must, of course, get proper treatment in the meantime. The importance of stressing the suffering caused, as well as the social and economic consequences of the disease, in education in schools has already been stressed on page 82.

The possibility of bilharzia infecting animals as well as people was raised in 1952 by some secondary school students in a school in the north of the Nile Delta, where bilharzia is widespread. It this were to happen, it would mean that the canals would always be infested with cercaria through the urine of such animals, even if people refrain from urinating in the canals. Their open-minded teacher helped them test this hypothesis. They put a field rat in a specially designed cage, where they could collect samples of its urine. The rat was infected with cercaria by the local doctor. Students took care of the rat and collected samples of the urine and looked for bilharzia eggs. Sure enough, for the first time, they discovered the presence of eggs in the rat's urine. When they reported their discovery to health officials, they were extremely disappointed when the experts laughed at them and excluded the possibility of the rat being infected with bilharzia. Now it is known that bilharzia infects other animals besides humans.

46

Carcinogenicity induced by Environmental Agents

F. DOMNGANG

Yaounde, Cameroun

In some parts of Africa and Asia the level of aflatoxin contamination of local foods is related to the incidence of liver cancer. Educational programmes should stress reference to this hazard which occurs in the environment. An understanding of the chemistry, biochemistry and biology associated with it would help to devise ways of minimizing the serious effects of these naturally occurring environmental carcinogens.

Aflatoxins are toxic compounds produced by some strains of the fungus *Aspergillus flavus* growing under warm, humid conditions on stored groundnuts, cereals and other foodstuffs usually found in many tropical areas. A WHO/FAO advisory group has suggested that the maximal concentration of aflatoxin permitted in foodstuff should be 30 µg/kg, but in many parts of Africa and Asia human staple foods may be found to have ten to a hundred times the recommended maximum.

Various experimental studies have indicated ways in which the problem might be tackled. Studies with animals show that conversion of aflatoxins in the body into more polar, and consequently more water soluble, metabolites (detoxification) results in their more rapid elimination from the body. However such studies have not so far resulted in ways of protecting humans against aflatoxin toxicity in the liver. Instead there has been a more pragmatic approach in which the following factors which prevent or inhibit the growth of *Aspergillus flavus* have been investigated.

During harvest, avoiding physical damage to peanuts and removing field soil from the peanut pods since *Aspergillus flavus* appears to be indigenous to the soil; the use of insecticides with harvest crops, despite the fact that they inhibit mould growth and consequent toxin production only for a short time.

During storage, drying rice within 48 hours of harvesting to less than 20% moisture; regulation of atmospheric gases for storage of peanuts (when either oxygen decreases or carbon dioxide increases, aflatoxin production decreases); storing cured and fresh meat below 5°C or 0°C for extra margin of safety.

In addition physical and chemical destruction of aflatoxins may be accomplished. For cereals or groundnuts, heating or pressure cooking destroys aflatoxins. Alternatively treatment of wet peanuts with sodium bicarbonate, methylamine or sodium oxychloride (bleaching powder) is effective. The effects of diet have also been considered in order to see if the rate of metabolic detoxification can be increased; for example vitamin C supplement in the guinea pig increases detoxification, and protein deficiency increases carcinogenic effects on rats. It is at least clear from such studies that individuals receiving poor, unbalanced diet are likely to be at greater risk.

From the educational point of view, the importance is to promote awareness of the problem.

47

Malaria

G. STOLTMAN
Hope College, Michigan, USA

Malaria is one of the most devastating diseases of the modern world. It is estimated that 300 million people each year are afflicted with it, and it has a tremendous impact upon many nations. Each year 3–4 million people die as a result of malaria, and in terms of morbidity and economic loss the toll is scarcely reached by any other disease. Efforts at controlling malaria have had, at best, only moderate success.

Scientific Knowledge

The chain of infection involves three components: first, the organism which causes the disease; second, the host organisms; and third, the way in which the causative agent is transmitted from one host to another. The organism responsible for malaria is a protozoan called *Plasmodium*. It has a complex life cycle involving two hosts. One is the female *Anopheles* mosquito. Infection of the second host, the human, occurs when the mosquito takes a meal of blood. The mosquito injects saliva containing anticoagulant into the person to prevent the blood clogging up its mouth and *Plasmodium* sporozoites pass into the new host in the saliva. Within thirty minutes the sporozoites reach the liver. Here asexual reproduction, schizogony, occurs and terminates in the release of merozoites into the blood.

A fever of unknown origin in an area endemic for malaria and "spiked" temperature charts, should always arouse suspicion of malaria. Diagnosis rests upon identification of the protozoan in blood films.

The aim of treatment is to eliminate the *Plasmodia* before they can cause too much tissue damage. Chloroquine is usually the drug of choice, although other drugs may be used. Chloroquine-resistant strains of *Plasmodium* have emerged in parts of Latin America, South-East Asia and Africa. In these cases, other drugs such as quinine must be used. Chloroquine and other anti-plasmodial drugs may also be used to prevent malaria.

Malaria is found primarily in the tropical and sub-tropical areas of the world. When a disease is found in a place all of the time it is said to be endemic in that area. Malaria is normally restricted to those areas where the *Anopheles* mosquito breeds. The *Anopheles* mosquito can be distinguished from other mosquitoes by its stance. *Anopheles* stands with its abdomen up whereas other mosquitoes have a more level stance. The female mosquito requires blood for her reproductive functions. The eggs are laid on still water and hatch in 2–3 days. The larvae and pupae remain just below the surface, using small breathing tubes to obtain air. After a few weeks the adult mosquitoes emerge.

Control Measures

Most control measures have been aimed at eradicating the mosquito. DDT has been used extensively and successfully. It is relatively inexpensive, an important consideration for countries with limited financial resources, but recently DDT has been banned in many countries because of its harmful effects on the ecology. Also some mosquitoes seem to be resistant to DDT. Other (more expensive) insecticides include malathion. Other means of killing mosquitoes include spraying water where mosquitoes lay their eggs, with substances such as oil, which prevents breathing tubes from reaching the air. Many animals such as frogs and fish, will feed on mosquito larvae, and the introduction of these animals into an area will substantially reduce the mosquito population.

The removal of mosquito breeding grounds can be achieved by draining areas of standing or still water, so that the mosquito is deprived of suitable places to breed.

Any measure which prevents a mosquito from biting, and transmitting the *Plasmodium* will be helpful. These include covering the skin as much as possible by long sleeves, trousers, etc. Another measure is to remain inside during the evening hours when mosquitoes are most active. Dwellings should have screens over windows and doors to prevent entry of mosquitoes, and insecticide sprays should be used to kill any which do get in. Also important is the isolation of malaria patients in rooms where mosquitoes cannot reach them. Other control methods focus on the destruction of the *Plasmodium* either with drugs or newer methods utilizing vaccines.

Control through Education

Education of at-risk communities increases the success rates of control. When people are made aware of the facts and can weigh the alternatives, they are more likely to have positive and effective responses.

The role of education in the fight against malaria is crucial. Past hopes and expectations of malaria eradication resulting from the use of pesticides have been unfulfilled. In addition these measures proved expensive. Simple and inexpensive measures carried out by communities can go a long way towards the goal of malaria extinction. But communities must know and understand the methods and reasons for the measures they take.

Lesson 1 should consider the life cycles of *Anopheles* and *Plasmodium* and the chain of transmission. In introducing the lesson, indicate the geographical distribution of malaria (most areas are tropical and in developing nations) and mention that increases in migration and air travel have led to cases of malaria outside the endemic areas.

Discuss the morbidity and mortality associated with malaria and indicate the social and economic effects of the mortality rates and also the effects of morbidity in terms of health costs and work days lost. Mention also that mortality is highest in children.

Describe the organisms and the life cycles step-by-step. Make sure the students understand where each stage occurs (in mosquito stomach, in human liver). Students should know which stage is transmitted from mosquito to human and which stage passes from human to mosquito. The students should appreciate the necessity for both vector and human host. If one is removed, the cycle is broken.

Indicate that the female *Anopheles* requires blood. Also describe the distinctive posture of *Anopheles*. Go through the habitat and life cycle of *Anopheles*. Emphasize the role of water – any still water, whether in ponds and lakes or in old oil drums, etc.

Plasmodium is transmitted in blood via a mosquito. Ask the students to consider other situations, not involving an insect, where *Plasmodium*-contaminated blood may be passed from one person to another. What is the significance of the absence of the mosquito? (Hint: Merozoites have been transmitted via contaminated syringes and needles and also in blood and serum used for transfusions.)

Why is it an advantage for *Plasmodium* to have the mosquito as the vector? (Hint: Mosquitoes fly around and can distribute the parasite over a large area. A mosquito will bite many people, increasing the rate of *Plasmodium* survival.)

Lesson 2 should consider malaria as a disease process and its treatment, present and future. The objectives should lead to an understanding how *Plasmodium* affects the human body; knowing the major symptoms of malaria; promoting familiarity with the treatment and prevention measures; and the efforts to produce a malaria vaccine.

When introducing the lesson begin by reviewing the chain of transmission and the *Plasmodium* life cycle. Then develop the lesson as follows:

(a) indicate that increased morbidity and mortality are associated with the very young and with persons already in poor health;

(b) go over the temperature chart, explaining why there is fever and why it is intermittent;

(c) indicate other symptoms, anaemia, splenomegaly, blackwater fever, and work through with the students the reasons for these symptoms, and mention also blockage of blood vessels and possible consequences;

(d) indicate that diagnosis is based on fever, especially if intermittent, and on identification of *Plasmodium* in blood smears;

(e) go over the drugs used for treatment and for prophylaxis; discuss the emergence of drug resistant strains and how these are being tackled;

(f) discuss vaccines and their purpose; explain how new techniques are being used to produce an anti-malaria vaccine.

In lesson 3, the key concepts are the social, economic and ecological aspects of control. Students should understand the principles of vector control; appreciate the need for education about malaria; recognize and understand the conflicts over DDT; and appreciate the economic and social problems of malaria. Develop the lesson as follows:

(a) go through the current methods for mosquito control; ask the students to suggest places, both natural and man-made, where still water may be found. Then ask for ways to deal with these breeding locations;

(b) consider insecticides, where they are used and what problems are associated with their use;

(c) discuss the effects of interrupting the *Plasmodial* life cycle at the following points: (i) entry into humans; (ii) migration to the liver; (iii) within erythrocytes; (iv) transmission to mosquito; indicate where control measures are being used or soon to be used and where they act in the cycle.

A useful activity is to get the students to read the following passage and then discuss the reasons for the increase in malaria in Brazil. Ask them how they would convince people of the benefits of having their house sprayed. Discuss how a disease like malaria affects not only the patient, but his family and the community. Ask the students why they think that education is an important factor in the fight against malaria.

Problems of malaria control

The jungle outpost in Brazil is at the front line of the war between mosquito and man. Well over 50% of the population has malaria, prompting the government to fight back with increasing quantities of DDT.

DDT has sunk into disrepute because of its damaging effect upon the ecology. However in developing countries, DDT is still the preferred insecticide. It is cheaper than alternatives, an important consideration for poor countries.

Sucam, a government organization, aims to keep 36 workers busy spraying DDT. They coat the inside walls of homes where mosquitoes like to sit. However, many people are so poor, they live in open-sided shelters with no walls. Health workers must therefore persuade them to put up burlap walls at the least.

People's ignorance obstructs DDT, even in many homes with walls. Many resent the need to spray twice a year. Walls need to be left to dry for three days after spraying, but many wash their walls straight away after the health worker has left, because they think the spraying makes their homes dirty. A lot of people do not realize that the mosquitoes carry malaria. They say it is the climate or gases.

48

Educating the "Educated" in Leprosy

I. NATH

All India Institute of Medical Sciences, New Delhi, India

Leprosy is a multifaceted disease which has been recognized at least since biblical times. In spite of the worthy attempts of devoted medical, religious and social personnel, leprosy still evokes a feeling of dread in the sufferer. Recent scientific advances in the understanding of the disease have, however, brought about many changes in the attitudes of medical and lay people towards leprosy patients.

Like the disease, teaching about leprosy needs to be multifaceted. The patients, the family and village concerned, religious leaders, health workers such as doctors and paramedical staff, and medical research workers are the people who require education. The last, but the most important are governments, which need to be motivated to handle leprosy as an integrated problem encompassing health, education, and rehabilitation. In India, every state has special leprosy units supported by the governments, religious and secular voluntary organizations and medical colleges, which screen and treat leprosy patients. Nevertheless, India has a quarter of the world's population of leprosy patients. Three-and-a-half million recorded cases of leprosy exist, in addition to as many undiagnosed patients. Recent advances in immunology and molecular biology have brought new insight into the understanding of leprosy.

This contribution attempts to draw attention to the approaches required to educate the "educated" about the basic problems of leprosy, and how such approaches may drastically reduce the consequences of the disease and contain it.

The problems in leprosy are many. The bacillus *M. leprae* has not been cultivated *in vitro*. It infects the human race predominantly, the mouse to a limited extent, the armadillo in an erratic manner, the monkey very rarely. Since it cannot be grown in the test tube, drug development has been hampered and indeed most drugs used today were originally designed to treat tuberculosis. In addition, the disfigurement caused by the disease discourages both medical and nursing personnel from handling the patient. Thus the education of the "educated" needs to be begun early.

Features of Leprosy in Medical Education

Leprosy shows a spectrum of clinical features ranging from the localized, single hypopigmented, paucibacillary tuberculoid leprosy patch to the generalized, multibacillary lepromatous leprosy. In addition to the skin, the nerves act as a reservoir for the leprosy bacilli. Currently it is thought that the wide spectrum in leprosy is due to the variation in the level of cellular defence mechanisms of the host and not to strain variation of the infecting organisms.

Leprosy predominantly affects the skin and nerves. Thus, when anatomy and neurophysiology are taught in medical schools leprosy can be considered as a topic for teaching. In addition to a brief mention when skin pigmentation and melanin formation are dealt with, the disease could be tackled during classes in neurophysiology and neuroanatomy. Leprosy patients could be used to demonstrate the superficial nerve trunks and their distribution. Nerve thickening, nerve tenderness and anaesthesia are the hallmarks of leprosy and early nerve involvement is a feature of the relatively resistant non-infectious tuberculoid leprosy. In a typical patient, the nerves in the vicinity of the lesion may be easily defined. Interestingly, it is the sensory nerve fibres that are first affected. Later, due to inflammation and demyelination, motor fibres are damaged, resulting in wasting of the muscles being supplied by the nerve. At this stage nerve conduction studies on the patient would define the electrophysiological defects and the retardation of conduction of electrical impulses along the pathway of the altered nerve.

During the second phase of paraclinical studies, leprosy can be considered in the disciplines of pathology and microbiology. Biopsy sections of skin lesions can be used to demonstrate the whole gamut of leprosy. In microbiology, students could study the slit smears of skin, after staining with the Ziehl-Nielsen stain.

When students are attending clinics, special efforts should be made to show patients with characteristics of all the varieties of leprosy. In addition special attention may be drawn to the episodic debilitating "reactions" that occur, including joint pains, fever and kidney involvement. Special teaching by experts in neurology and renal diseases would reiterate the multi-organ involvement by this disease and the multidisciplinary therapeutic approach required to treat leprosy.

In the third phase of education, medical students and nurses should observe the treatment of the sequelae and complications of the disease. Physiotherapy, and surgery for rehabilitation of atrophied muscles, are the main aspects to be considered. In recent years advances in tendon transplants, plastic surgery for disfigured noses and earlobes, and eyebrow transplants for denuded eyebrows have greatly facilitated the return of the patient to normal life. Hand surgery, too, is a challenging exercise for the skilled surgeon and physiotherapist.

Finally, the greatest challenge to society is the integration of the patient into the community by well thought out occupational therapy. It is an inspiration to see stubbed hands and toeless feet being used to manufacture carpets, garments, and baskets, or to grow food, to raise cows, and so on.

Research Training in Immunology and Molecular Biology

Advances made in modern research in the last two decades have revolutionized our understanding of leprosy. After centuries of incarceration in dark caves, leprosy has emerged as a fascinating intellectual challenge to the modern research worker.

The renaissance in our understanding of leprosy began in immunology and the training in the immunology of leprosy may be at graduate or post-graduate level.

The recent advent of recombinant DNA technology has made possible cDNA probes coding for *M. leprae* antigens. These are at the stage of being investigated for use. Although this branch of discipline is at its infancy in India, its potential is enormous for vaccine production where there is a shortage of bacilli as is the case with leprosy. The cDNA probes can be cloned in vectors to provide large quantities of antigens required for vaccines.

49

Education about Common Diseases caused by Parasitic Roundworms

N. P. SALAZAR and D. F. HERNANDEZ
University of the Philippines

When deciding on which diseases to include in the course of science teaching, it is important to include those which are the most prevalent among the children in the communities in which they live, and this will often include common parasitic roundworms. The following are the problems related to infection:

- the lack of knowledge about modes of infection;
- the lack of appreciation of what are healthful practices;
- the susceptibility of children, due to their modes of behaviour;
- the lack of health consciousness;
- the social aspect of crowding.

Further problems are the nutritional situation, stunted growth, poor motivation (for example, in school work) and general debility.

It is suggested that the following strategies would be appropriate in both formal and informal educational systems.

1. Adopting a positive approach to overcome successfully the disturbance in the living system.
2. Explaining how to overcome the disturbance in the system through curative measures.
3. Explaining about preventive measures and personal hygiene.
4. Using specific situations common to the children's local experience.
5. Teaching the biological aspects of the disease for a deeper understanding.
6. Using analogies to emphasize certain points (for example, how much

253

rice is consumed by *Ascaris* in one year in order to illustrate how infected children are energy-deprived).

7. Explaining the consequences to one's productivity when imbalances continue in the system.

In any educational process, it is important to involve the community. Parents' support should always be obtained; information should be provided in brief, concrete ways (for example with the use of posters); sanitary measures involving the whole community should be stressed. In order to facilitate changes of attitude, a participatory approach should be used; there should be service orientation of workers to extend the educational work, regular visits over an extended period and visits by leaders of the educational project in order to show concern.

PART VIII

Other Papers

Introduction

It was inevitable that at Bangalore some interesting contributions would be made which did not fit precisely into the categories designated by the various sections of this book and it is appropriate to include them here.

The first of these is a paper on "Health Emphasis in Biology Examinations" which includes some imaginative questions used in Australia and this is followed by a few examples of examination questions used in the Science-in-Society project in the UK.

Training teachers is another important topic and is represented first by a description of teacher training in the UK from Trefor Williams and, secondly, by an account of inservice training in Australia by Rex Meyer.

A short paper on medicinal plants reminds us of the differences between western medicine and what is traditional in many countries and how what is valuable in traditional medicine should not be lost.

A paper by K. Imahori considers a case for the integration of oriental and western medicine.

The section finishes with a health education check-list and some suggestions for a guide-book to health.

50

Health Emphasis in Biology Examinations

G. R. MEYER

Macquarie University, Australia

Examinations can have a profound influence on what is taught in schools. This chapter is included, despite the author's opening disclaimer about the value of public examinations in general, because it contains some interesting examples of the kind of question which was set in New South Wales in Australia during the 1970s.

In Australia it is generally agreed amongst educationalists that public examinations at school level are bad things and should be abolished if possible. Most, in fact, have been abolished but some States, including NSW, have at least retained a Higher School Certificate examination as some measure of achievement at the end of secondary schooling and to assist with selection for further studies. While most educators are uncomfortable with this system a reasonable alternative has yet to be evolved and so a major effort is made to ensure that the examination does have some positive influence on teaching and learning. Biology examiners in particular make an effort in this regard and the emphasis given to health education is a good example.

Inspection of Higher School Biology examination papers for the 5 years 1973 to 1977 in New South Wales indicates the type of approach adopted.[1] Incidentally all papers inspected included major blocks of multiple-choice questions; some questions requiring answers in one to five lines (the number of lines required always being nominated) and two or three questions requiring answers of about one page in length.

In the first place there was a generally even spread of questions on those routines of health usually addressed by biologists. These included questions about genetic disorders; parasitic diseases and their control; nutritional problems; environmental pollution and its health implications; and abnormalities in the functioning of body organs such as heart, lungs, etc.

Secondly, however, questions on these basic issues usually required more than mere recall of facts and involved some degree of interpretation or problem solving.

Some typical examples from the area of nutrition include the following:

40. A person who is advised to go on a low-fat diet goes into a supermarket and sees two milk products whose composition is listed as follows:

	Product I	Product II
Protein	28.5%	37.5%
Lactose	37.3%	50.7%
Butterfat	26%	1%
Minerals	5.3%	5.3%
Calories per gram	5.13	4.5

Which of the two products, I or II, should he choose? Give a reason.

(1973, question 40)

12. The table below gives the composition and energy value of a selection of foods.

Food	Composition (g per 100 g)			Kilojoules per 100 g
	Protein	Fat	Carbohydrate	
Sugar	trace	trace	100	1 638
Chocolate	9	38	55	2 478
Oranges	1	trace	6	113
Cheese	26	31	trace	1 638
Wheatmeal biscuits	10	21	66	2 016
Sardines	20	23	trace	1 218
Peas (dried)	6	trace	17	661

A mountaineer who plans an energetic 3 day trek wants to minimize the weight of his food rations. His food pack for the trip should consist of –

(A) chocolate only, because it provides the most energy per unit mass.
(B) cheese only, because it is a high energy food and also contains the most protein per unit mass.
(C) Chocolate, cheese and oranges, since these contain balanced amounts of needed foods.
(D) 200 g of each food listed.   (. . . . .)

(1974, question 12)

17. It has been shown that rats trained to eat their entire daily food ration in one to two hours, gain more weight than rats eating their ration over frequent intervals. It was further demonstrated that these trained rats increased by 25 times the rate at which their fatty tissue built up.

The significance of this research for weight watchers, is –

(A) concentrating a large part of daily food intake into one meal may cause increase in fatty deposits.
(B) restriction of the intake of high carbohydrate foods is an outmoded way to avoid overweight.
(C) to lose weight, eat as much as you like, as often as you can.
(D) nil, because the metabolism of rats is completely different from that of man.   (. . . . .)

(1975, question 17)

In addition, the context of health issues was frequently emphasized, sometimes by means of giving literary quotes or referring to current newspaper articles. The following examples from the area of nutrition are representative.

33. Mark Twain once wrote:

> "Part of the secret of success in life is to eat what you like and let the food fight it out inside."

> This statement is unacceptable today. What two features, based on scientific principles, must be taken into consideration in advising an overweight person about suitable diet?

(1975, question 33)

38. Read the following extract from a newspaper article.

INQUIRY INTO BREAD

The Minister for Health, Mr Waddy, said today he would make immediate inquiries into reports that iron and vitamin B were being added to bread in a NSW town as part of a medical experiment.

It was reported in yesterday's "National Times" that the iron and vitamins were being added to all bread made in Bourke, without the townspeople's knowledge.

There have been reports in the United States recently that excess iron can be fatal to some people.

It has been blamed as a cause of cirrhosis of the liver, pancreatic damage, diabetes and heart failure.

(*The Sun,* Monday, 25th February, 1974)

Give one argument for and one argument against the "experiment" as reported in the above article.

(1975, question 38)

Wherever possible students were encouraged to apply biological principles in solving problems arising from previously unseen situations directly or indirectly involving health issues. In the following three examples, the first two (baldness, detergents) aim to test problem-solving skills in new contexts and the third (about a space ship) probes in part for an understanding that health depends on total control of all aspects of the human environment.

EH-J

29. Study the following extract from a newspaper article published in 1972.

NOW SMOKING CAN CAUSE BALDNESS

AAP-REUTER, NEW YORK, WEDNESDAY

To prevent baldness, avoid smoking excessively and emotional upheaval, according to a book published in New York this week.

Excessive intake of coffee and salt can also encourage baldness, syndicated columnist Marylou McKenna wrote in her book, *Revitalize Yourself*.

However, surgeons in West Germany and Switzerland are doing research on an operation which would remedy baldness caused by tension.

In the operation, termed epicraniotomy, incisions are made across the top of the forehead in an unnoticeable skin fold, at the back of the neck and near each ear.

This helps relieve constriction of the blood vessels – caused by emotional tension – and helps restore impaired circulation to hair roots, the doctors say.

Hanging one's head over the bed just after waking and the massaging the scalp for three minutes is also recommended by the writer of the "Stay Younger Longer" column.

The book noted that cigarette smoke dehydrates . . . scalp and facial tissues, causing balding and wrinkles.

(*The Sun*, Thursday, Dec, 1972)

Restate in your own words any one hypothesis, implied in the article, to explain the cause of baldness. Describe an experiment that could be undertaken to test your hypothesis.

(1976, question 29)

50. The following report appeared recently in a popular science magazine:

"A debate continues about the effect of enzyme-detergents on the hands of people using these for general washing purposes. Some reports allege there is a risk of these detergents causing dermatitis and other diseases.

An important study was undertaken with a group of about 7,000 women. The scientists conducting the study organized 4,000 of them to use enzyme-containing products, while the remainder were given non-enzyme products. The subjects used the products for all cleaning jobs, not just for washing clothes but were unaware of the product they were using.

The investigation was carried out for about five months, during which time the medical condition of the subjects' hands was examined. The overall condition of the hands was given a score on an ordinal scale. In an extensive series of five tests no significant difference was found between subjects.

The team also decided to see if people who were pre-disposed to poor hand conditions reacted differently from those with normal hands. Again the enzyme and non-enzyme detergents gave the same reaction."

List the features of this investigation which might be considered significant in assessing the effect of enzyme-detergents on users' hands.

(1973, question 50)

35. The diagram shows the plan of a spaceship which has been designed to sustain three people for 2 years in an orbit around Mars.

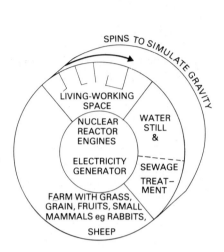

The life support system has been designed to be as close as possible to that on planet Earth. It is a small ecosystem, with soil, air, plants, and animals.

Assume that all the mechanical equipment works perfectly.

Suggest how the people on the ship would have to manage the ecosystem. Point out possible situations that could alter the ecosystem in a way that could endanger the lives of the astronauts. How might these situations be avoided or remedied?

(1976, question 35)

The previous example about the spaceship leads to a further principle stressed by the examination questions, namely that the concept of health extends beyond the health of mankind as such to the health of other organisms and to the health of the whole ecosystem. The following examples are representative of this approach:

49. "Perhaps the most regrettable consequence of oil spills at sea is the toll of life they inevitably take – fish, sea birds, aquatic mammals, marine plants and plankton are all poisoned and often die. Now, however, the US Navy is experimenting with several varieties of marine bacteria that actually consume oil, and the hope is that they may prove a highly effective agent in reducing the damage from future oil spills."

(a) Suggest a reason why bacteria might be considered suitable organisms to introduce.
(b) Why would experimentation be necessary before introducing the marine bacteria to the oil slick?

(1973, question 49)

47. Read the following extracts from a newspaper article.

PRIVATE AIRCRAFT 'THREAT' TO ANIMALS

CANBERRA, Monday. – Light aircraft entering Australia posed a threat to Australia's freedom from foot-and-mouth disease, the Opposition spokesman on primary industry, transport and shipping, Mr A. Street, said today.

Many privately owned and chartered aircraft were being used for flights to South-East Asian countries and Indonesia.

"It is of critical importance that they receive the same treatment on entering Australia as do commercial flights," he said.

People walking off planes here, without using formalin footbaths, placed Australia "on the edge of a volcano," particularly if they had spent any time walking in disease-infested fields in Bali.

The Sydney Morning Herald, Tuesday, November 13th, 1973

In the last century there was little need to take such precautions as formalin footbaths for people and stock arriving in Australia from overseas.

(a) Suggest a reason why it was unnecessary.

_____

(b) Suggest another way that precautions could be taken now to protect the people and stock.

_____

(1974, question 47)

Finally, health aspects were included incidentally and by implication in many questions probing for very broad understandings of the role of science in society. The two examples which follow are typical of this approach.

54. It has been stated that:
> "In school biology, discussion of human nutrition, biological warfare, agricultural chemicals and pesticides, and population growth is more crucial than the anatomy of an earthworm or the structure of a cell."
> Professor L. C. Birch
> *Sydney Morning Herald*, 13th July, 1972.
> Do you agree with this? Select one of the topics referred to and justify your answer.

(1973, question 54)

36. Sir John Kendrew in the journal *New Scientist* (September 1974) stated:

> "I feel that national boundaries in general are bad, and that anything which can break them down is good, and international science is one method."

Suggest two areas of biological endeavour which have led to better international understanding and co-operation. Explain how they have aided in breaking down national boundaries.

(1976, question 36A)

In answer to these two questions candidates had an opportunity to include examples from the area of health and most took advantage of this opportunity.

The use of the public examinations in this way led during the seventies to a major shift in emphasis in the teaching of biology throughout the State. While this approach is perhaps less marked in current examination papers the need for an "artificial" incentive via examination questions is not so necessary as a decade ago. Most teachers now appreciate that the facts of biology are not enough in themselves. Most also appreciate that the development of inquiry and problem-solving skills has little significance unless these skills are applied in the solution of socially meaningful problems, including aspects of health. There is a heightened awareness among biology teachers of the importance of interrelating the aims of the biology programme with those of health studies.

Examinations have proved to be one effective way of helping ensure that health education is developed through biology programmes. Another has been the production of suitable resources. A third has been through inservice education (see pages 271–279).

Reference

1. NSW Department of Education *Higher School Certificate Examination Science Six Period Trial Course Biology 1973, 1974* and *1975*.
    NSW Department of Education *Higher School Certificate Examination Science 2 Unit Course 4 Unit Doublestrand Course Biology 1976*.

    NSW Department of Education *Higher School Certificate Examination Science 2 Unit Course Biology 1977*.

51

Examination Questions in the Science-in-Society Project

J. L. LEWIS
Malvern College, England

Multiple choice questions are, on the whole, unsuitable for social questions. The imaginative questions from Australia in the previous chapter show what can be set. We include below examples of some of the questions involving aspects of health and medicine which have been set in the Science-in-Society examination in the UK. (Marks awarded in brackets.)

1. "Health is too important a matter to be left to doctors alone." Discuss this with reference to
   (*a*) the greatest successes of curative medicine in the past hundred years; [4]
   (*b*) other causes of improvements in health during the same period; [4]
   (*c*) how you would set about research to determine the significance of factors other than curative medicine in improving health; [4]
   (*d*) the suggestion that you are as well as you think you are; [4]
   (*e*) how priorities for the health service should be established. [4]
   June 1981

2. Birth Control is a very controversial subject. Write an essay on it bringing out its importance to individuals, its importance to nations, the dangers associated with it and the different moral viewpoints held on it. [20]
   June 1981

3.   **Either**   Suggest and comment briefly on **five** environmental factors which can affect your health. Your comments should make clear what an individual can do to avoid disease.   [5 × 4]

   Or   In 1900 life expectancy in the United States was 47 years; now it is 73. Outline the chief causes and the chief consequences of this change.   [20]

June 1982

4.   (a) Explain why the proportion of old people in our society has increased and will continue to do so.   [7]

   (b) What special help do old people need, and should they receive it from public organizations or from their relations and other private helpers?   [7]

   (c) What will be the effects of increased expectation of life combined with the likelihood of a lowering of the normal age of retirement?   [6]

June 1983

5.   Four of the most important threats to good health are lack of exercise, unwise choice of diet, excesses of such things as tobacco, drugs or alcohol, and accidents. Write a paragraph on each of these, discussing how these dangers affect members of a developed society and the best ways to avoid them.   [4 × 5]

June 1983

6.   Compare the problems involved in the setting up of a National Health Service in a developed and a developing country.   [20]

June 1984

7.   (a) Give a brief outline of the way in which inoculation and vaccination were brought into use in England.   [7]

   (b) What are the arguments for and against the immunization of babies against whooping cough?   [7]

   (c) To what extent do you think that, in the public interest, society should limit an individual's freedom of action in matters of health?   [6]

June 1984

8.   A survey recently revealed what percentages of the French nation are the cause of the cost of various proportions of the French medical services. The survey divides the whole French nation into four categories, A, B, C or D. The figures quoted in the survey are given overpage.

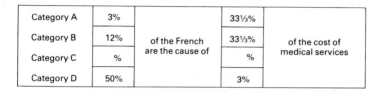

Category A	3%	of the French are the cause of	33⅓%	of the cost of medical services
Category B	12%		33⅓%	
Category C	%		%	
Category D	50%		3%	

(a) What are the missing figures in Category C?   [1]
(b) What percentage of the French use more than twice their average share?   [2]
(c) What percentage use less than their average share?   [2]
(d) Jean le Brun is one of the 50% who use only 3% of the services. How would you counter his claim that he should be given a tax rebate to repay what he had paid for nothing?   [5]
(e) What do you think are the main groups of people to be found in Category A?   [5]
(f) If you were in charge of a campaign to reduce avoidable calls upon the medical services, suggest with reasons two or three of the chief points that you would make in order to persuade people to co-operate.   [5]

June 1985

9.   In the USA there are HMOs (Health Maintenance Organizations). You pay them a lump sum, and in return they maintain your health for the following year by meeting your medical needs, including any necessary hospital treatment.

If you were setting up an HMO and planning a scale of charges reflecting the probable costs, what enquiries would you make into the life style of applicants? Indicate the broad principles on which you would assess risk without trying to quantify them.   [20]

June 1985

52

Training of Teachers

T. WILLIAMS

Southampton University, UK

Trefor Williams is the Director of the Health Education Unit in the Department of Education of Southampton University. This chapter is included as it gives an account of an attempt in England and Wales to revive the interest of teacher education establishments in health education, a topic on which experience elsewhere is limited.

Early in 1981 the Health Education Council (England and Wales) invited the Health Education Unit, University of Southampton, to undertake a research and development project to discover what was happening regarding health education in initial teacher education and to develop materials and strategies for the re-establishment and resuscitation of this area of work as a viable and important part of the professional preparation of teachers. Those associated with the development of school health education have become seriously concerned with the apparent decline in the status and importance of health education as a part of the curriculum of student teachers. Traditionally, health education has always been a small but important segment of their work but this has declined markedly over the past decade.

The Investigation

In order to provide a useful base line for developments, three national surveys were conducted. First, in schools, a 12½% random postal survey of all primary and secondary schools to find out whether schools included health education in their curriculum, whether health education was a valued part of their school work and whether teachers thought health education should be included in teacher training. Secondly, in teacher education establishments, a postal survey of all establishments and a visit to a third of them to clarify the position of health education and to identify the most useful materials for further developments. Thirdly, among a 16% stratified sample of students to clarify students' expectations concerning health education and their own teaching, and to find out whether students felt well-equipped to teach health education.

The results of the survey may be summarized as follows:

(a) Over 90% of schools said they include health education in their curriculum and strongly supported the view that health education should be a small core element in initial teacher education.

(b) Less than 25% of teacher education institutions include health education as a core element for students, but 63% of them offered some kind of health education input, but this varies from as little as 1 hour to 50 hours or more.

(c) Over 90% of students believed that schools have a responsibility for including health education in their curriculum and over 80% would welcome the opportunity of contributing to it. But less than half of the students considered their preparation was adequate for such a task.

The basic ambiguity is that, whereas schools by and large are attempting to develop programmes of health education for their pupils, few teacher education institutions appear to be taking the matter seriously in terms of preparing students for such activities.

Developments

Writing groups involving staff from over 70% of the teacher education institutions have helped to produce a considerable array of materials, concentrating in particular on teaching methods, which include small group discussion, investigations, role-play, simulations, gaming, etc.

The materials can be used flexibly to construct a "course" in health education ranging from 6 to 80 hours' duration, or can be readily incorporated into existing courses (education, professional studies), or into specialist curriculum areas such as science, home economics, physical education or primary school science. Each unit, while setting out to develop knowledge and skills at the students' own level, also contains components related to school-based materials.

Individual workshops contain comprehensive tutors' notes, student readers where appropriate, activity sheets and other forms of guidance for both tutors and students, including reference and resource lists.

Foundation Unit – Unit 1: Health Education Awareness Day

This unit comprises several interactive workshops which address themselves to issues and questions basic to school health education.

1. *20 healthy statements* – which explore the broad scope of health education and require the students to examine their own definitions of

health. This activity requires students to work together in pairs and in small groups and to articulate their ideas of health and health education.

2. *The school as a health-promoting community* – This workshop aims to sensitize students to the responsibility that schools and teachers have regarding the health and well-being of pupils. While much emphasis is placed upon the taught health education curriculum, this needs to be supported by the hidden curriculum of the school. The method employed by the workshop includes personal reflections which are shared with a small group, group discussions concerning school organization and a role-play.

3. *Towards a planned school health education programme* – This sets out to demonstrate to students the need for a planned curriculum in health education based upon the needs of pupils. The workshop also explores what the main strands of health education might be and the various influences which affect the health behaviour of children of different ages. The methods are based upon negotiations between groups of students considering the health needs of specific age groups of children.

Each of the workshops includes readers and other material for students and also suggests the mounting of a small exhibition of available school-based and pupil materials in health education.

This unit – as with all units – also contains an evaluation component related to the responses of both students and tutors.

One of the main difficulties faced by the project is the great shortage of time available in the teacher education curriculum – particularly in the context of the Postgraduate Certificate in Education (PGCE), which is the major route towards teacher qualifications for secondary school teachers. This is a 36-week course which usually includes a 10–12 week teaching practice module. The Health Education Awareness Day is particularly useful here in sensitizing students to some of the issues and problems faced by school health education.

Core and Option Material

The further units include "core" and "option" material developed by the project. For each unit there is a "key workshop" and these might form the basis for a core course, but the additional material in each unit is designed so that the material can be used in a variety of curriculum contexts. The units are:

Unit 2 School and Community
Unit 3 Growth and Development
Unit 4 Relationships
Unit 5 Drug Education

EH–K*

Unit 6 Mental Health
Unit 7 Fitness and Nutrition
Unit 8 Sexuality
Unit 9 Safety and First Aid

Units 10–13 are designed for use in the context of specialist subjects in biology, home economics, physical education and primary science. The details of the units are as follows:

UNIT 2   SCHOOL AND COMMUNITY
          Key workshop   **1 Community profile**
                             2 Agencies
                             3 How change is brought about
                             4 Life stages
                             5 Teachers as role models in school
                                and society
                             6 Community and school – primary workshop
                             7 Community and school – secondary workshop

UNIT 3   GROWTH AND DEVELOPMENT
          Key workshop   **1 Similarities and differences**
                             2 Perspective on growth and development I
                             3 Perspective on growth and development II
                             4 Influences on growth and development
                             5 School health education and growth and development

UNIT 4   RELATIONSHIPS
          Key workshop   **1 The professional role of the teacher**
                             2 Relationship building skills
                             3 Body image and relationships
                             4 Self-esteem and relationships
                             5 Pastoral role of the teacher
                             6 School-based materials on relationships

UNIT 5   DRUG EDUCATION
          Key workshop   **1 Understanding drug taking**
                             2 Drug education in primary schools
                             3 Drug education in secondary schools

UNIT 6   MENTAL HEALTH
          Key workshop   **1 Perceptions of mental health**
                             2 Stress
                             3 Coping with stress
                             4 Self-esteem
                             5 Mental illness
                             6 Mental health – the influence of school
                                – what can school do?

UNIT 7   FITNESS AND NUTRITION
          Key workshop   **1 Eating and exercise and its relationship to health**
                             2 Influences
                             3 Implications for teaching in
                                (a) primary schools
                                (b) secondary schools

UNIT 8   SEXUALITY
            Key workshop   1   Questions children ask
            Key workshop   2   The current debate
                             3   Changing families (genogram)
                             4   Gender role
                             5   Human growth and development
                                      (i) Sexuality in formative years 0–9
                                      (ii) Adolescence

UNIT 9   SAFETY AND FIRST AID

UNIT 10   HEALTH EDUCATION AND PRIMARY SCHOOL SCIENCE
            Workshop   1   Ourselves (5–7 years)
                        2   Growing
                        3   How growth begins
                        4   Keeping safe
                        5   Water – environment

UNIT 11   HEALTH EDUCATION AND BIOLOGY

UNIT 12   HEALTH EDUCATION AND PHYSICAL EDUCATION
            Workshop   1   What relationship has health education to physical
                             education
                        2   Exercise: The evidence for and against
                        3   Theory into practice
                        4   Individual needs
                        5   Lifestyles
                        6   The physical education teacher as a role model of
                             health
                        7   Safety and the physical education teacher
                        8   Hygiene and posture
                        9   The role of the non-specialist physical educationalist in
                             health education in the primary school

UNIT 13   HEALTH EDUCATION AND HOME ECONOMICS

Reference

Health Education in Schools and Teacher Education Institutions, D. T. Williams and J. Roberts, 1985, published by the Health Education Unit, University of Southampton.

53

Inservice Education in New South Wales

G. R. MEYER
Macquarie University, Australia

School teachers are in the main well-educated, intelligent, highly motivated professional people. Unfortunately inservice programmes for
teachers frequently overlook these obvious facts and conclude that
teachers must be continually exposed to elaborate, mandatory programmes of re-education to ensure effective professionalism. Actually the
converse is true. If teachers can teach others, and most can do so or they
would be in some other job, then it is almost axiomatic that they can teach
themselves. What is needed are devices to help them work out their
professional needs and the availability of resources to meet these needs.

In New South Wales there is growing awareness that this is the case and
while traditional "withdrawal" inservice activities continue to flourish, they
do so side by side with school-focused activities.

One of the devices becoming more popular in New South Wales is the
self-diagnostic check-list to help teachers identify those areas of strong
professionalism and those areas that could benefit by further professional
development.

A typical check-list might require teachers to rate themselves on a three
or five point scale on levels of achievement of a list of carefully defined
professional competencies. One such list[1] groups these competencies
under the following headings:

1. Standard of general education
2. Practical philosophy of education
3. General teaching skills
4. Professional development
5. Development of an optimal physical environment
6. Interpersonal relationships
7. Contributions to teaching improvement
8. Development of future teachers

277

Similar check-lists exist for departments or sections within a school or for a whole school. A check-list to assess the climate of a whole school could perhaps be organized under headings something as follows:

1. Aims and objectives of the programme
2. Decision-making
3. Interrelationships between members of staff
4. The curriculum
5. Morale of the students
6. Staff responsibilities and induction
7. Staff expectations, teaching loads and promotions
8. Communications
9. Resources
10. Parental links
11. Community links
12. The learning environment

Each category may contain up to ten competencies. Under the heading "curriculum", for example, competencies could include writing objectives, selecting subject matter, designing teaching methods and so on.

It is easy to see how such check-lists could be readily adapted to the requirements of health education. Teachers in biology could immediately check off their degree of success in integrating health education elements; in testing the achievement of health education objectives; in devising appropriate health education strategies; in applying basic biological principles in the solution of problems in health education; in liaising with the community on health issues and so on.

Once weaknesses are diagnosed, alert and forward-thinking teachers can readily tap into the multiplicity of resources for professional development available throughout the State. They can attend self-selected courses; undertake programmes of reading; attend appropriate conferences; talk with fellow teachers; seek advice from consultants and so on. Self-motivated and self-directed staff development programmes of this nature are maximally effective.

Conclusion

In New South Wales the holistic nature of the Health programme is becoming increasingly apparent to teachers. Biology teachers in particular perceive this and are increasingly committed to fostering the aims of health studies through biology lessons. This heightened awareness has emerged because of two decades of development through forward-thinking syllabus design; the availability of suitable resources; enlightened policies in public examining and school-focused inservice education concentrating on diagnosis of individual needs and the challenge of self-directed staff development.

Reference

1. Meyer, G. R. (with Jenkins C. and Chan, E.) in *Minicourse M48. Diagnosis of Organizational Needs in Education (Processes of teaching and learning — a series of manuals based on minicourses presented by the Centre for Advancement of Teaching, Macquarie University)* Sydney Centre for Advancement of Teaching, Macquarie University, 1978.

54

Incorporating Medicinal Plants into Health Education

M. E. ADDY

University of Ghana

In many parts of the world, such as Africa, traditional herbal medicine is still an important practice. Indeed, it has attracted the attention of scientists and doctors, many of whom now see much greater potential in it than they did before. For these reasons knowledge of medicinal plants and their uses should be included as topics in health education.

Empiricism characterizes the practice of herbal medicine. In fact, there is very little that one can describe as scientific in its practice. The herbalist uses no systematic classification of plant material and recognition is gained by experience. The dose is usually not standard because, even though the volume of a concoction to be taken may be stated, the concentration is likely to vary from one preparation to another. Once the preparation is given, preserving the medication at home is difficult, and one usually has to keep warming or boiling the extract made in order to keep it from spoilage. This process is likely to affect the concentration and nature of the therapeutic agent.

When a herbalist states that a particular plant material is used to treat a certain disease, the information has been handed down to him by his predecessor. He certainly knows which plant is for which disease. He knows that the woman with the abdominal pain will feel better when she takes a cupful of a particular plant preparation; but it is very unlikely that he knows what is causing the abdominal pain, what that plant preparation does to make her feel better, what else it is doing to the rest of her body and whether she will develop any other ailment because of it, let alone what to do should such a thing develop.

When a clinic prescribes insulin for a patient, it is done knowing that the patient is diabetic and that the diabetes is insulin-dependent. A known amount of insulin is prescribed for injection and how frequent the injections should be: the effects on the body are known as well as details of any side-effects which might develop; it is known what to do if the patient is returned to the clinic in a coma.

The difference between the practices of the herbalists and the workers in the clinic lies in the scientific work done by the pharmaceutical companies and the training given. Yet it is still possible for men and women to maintain their health to some extent by using the plants around them and this could be extended if there were to be a scientific approach to these traditional medicines.

Incorporation into School Syllabuses

A teacher making a conscious effort to educate students on some aspects of medicinal plants can use existing courses. During biology teaching some of the plants chosen for study might include medicinal plants in order to generate a more positive attitude towards their use against disease. What is being advocated here is an introduction to and a sustained interest in local medicinal plants so that students in the health-related sciences will almost automatically and constantly be mindful of their existence and potential.

One topic in the detailed syllabus of the West African School Certificate Science course is "Man as a Living Organism" and one section deals with Man's dependence on plants, and the notes emphasize photosynthesis and food chains. The contribution of medicinal plants to health could so easily be incorporated here. The point is that the avenue for incorporating medicinal plants into health education does already exist in school syllabuses.

Substantiating the Herbalists' Claims

It is of course imperative that the claims of the herbalists be substantiated. There is a need for institutions where scientific work can be done on herbal medicines and it is encouraging that the Scientific, Technical and Research Committee of the OAU has recommended such an institution. It will then be important to see that the knowledge acquired is incorporated into health education at all levels.

55

Oriental and Modern Western Medicine: The Case for Integration

Osaka University, Japan

It is uncertain when health education started in Japan, but Shinto, a unique traditional religion of this country, certainly influenced health care to some extent. "Sake", a kind of liqueur which is made from rice, is used in Shinto's ritual praying for health. "Sake is the best of all medicine" is a phrase sometimes heard.

Buddhism was introduced from China via Korea in AD 552 and attracted a large number of followers among highly educated people. As a result many temples were built in the Nara period (during the 70 years after AD 710 when Nara was the capital city of Japan, and Chinese culture was introduced). Among those temples, the Temple Yakushiji played the most noteworthy role in health education during this period, because the temple was the first Japanese institution for medical treatment and education. The name Yakushiji means "Pharmaceutical Teacher Temple"; there was a big herb garden there, where Kampow treatment (the use of herbs) and the training of Kampow doctors were performed.

Modern medicine is said to have had its origin in Japan with the translation of John Adam Kulmos' book *Ontleekundige Tafelen* by Genpaku Sugita in 1774. Seisyu Hanaoka in the early nineteenth century was noted for his invention of a general anaesthesia termed Tsusen-san, made from mixed herbs including *Aconitum*. He developed surgery, integrating oriental and western methods. Aided by Dutch, Danish and, particularly, German doctors a tradition of western (or "modern" as it is termed) medicine was built up. This was reinforced after World War II under the influence of American medical science.

Recently, however, old medical practices have flourished again in Japan, and now acupuncturists, moxa cauterizers, massagers and bonesetters are coming more and more into prominence in our society. Drugstores now usually sell both chemical and Kampow medicines, and laboratories of Kampow consultants are even occasionally attached to some of those stores. Kampow consultants are usually licensed as pharmacists, since today almost all of the pharmaceutical colleges have curricula that include Kampow and herbalism.

One of the major reasons for the revived interest in older traditions of medicine and health education related to it has been the problems caused by side-effects of modern drugs. For example, a well-known instance of the side-effect of a chemical is related to corticosteroid (corticoid) which is effective in the treatment of rheumatic arthritis. The corticoid, appropriately synthesized, is usually prescribed to patients with rheumatic diseases, as well as some with nephrosis or even with bronchiolar cancer. A remarkable ameliorative effect is found with the substance, but, on the other hand, the application must not be interrupted, otherwise the symptoms develop again. But with the process of continued application the patient develops the so-called "moon-face" (where the face of the patient becomes swollen) and death may inadvertently supervene. Oriental practitioners, on the other hand, are generally convinced that a curing process has to be very mild, takes rather a long time, and that side-effects will usually not occur, if the application dose is appropriate and the treatment given by an experienced oriental practitioner. However, it is true that many diseases declared "incurable" by oriental medicine are in fact curable by western medicine. Accordingly, it is good that western medicine has been more respected and promoted in Japan during this century.

It is interesting to see that in the People's Republic of China, too, they are endeavouring to accomplish the amalgamation of oriental and western medicine. For example, western medical treatment is always made after a diagnosis of cancer, but simultaneously Kampow practices and acupunctures are applied as well as the operation and cancer treatment with chemicals. Extracts from *Coliolus* sp. (a mushroom belonging to the Polyporales) and *Menispermum* sp. (belonging to the Menispermaceae among the Ranales) are usually used as carcinostatic herbs in China. It is well known that the extract of *Menispermum* is most effective in the treatment of lung and larynx cancer, though its effective substance, or medical mechanism, are quite unknown to date. Apparently medicine in China is more practical and pragmatic than purely scientific.

The general need of integrating oriental and western medicine has repeatedly been emphasized in modern societies, and a good example of the value of such integration is found in mechanisms of acupuncture treatment.

By acupuncture treatment neurofibre paralysis or ganglionoplegic effects can be detected. The first application of this anaesthetic effect to surgical procedures started in 1958 during an appendicitis operation. In the following 30 years around 5,000 examples were tried in China among which almost as many as 90% were successful. According to these results, patients continue to be without pain for about 20 hours after application, their blood pressure is usually stable, and no side-effects occur at all. Naturally these patients can be restored to health much faster than those who have had chemical anaesthesia. It must be assumed that some kind of neural substance, the chemical structure of which resembles that of morphine, is secreted from some part of the brain during acupuncture. This hormonal substance was named "endorphin" in 1978. The substance reacts strongly with the morphine receptors, and as a result doctors can perform operations without further anaesthetic.

For the promotion of medical sciences in order to rescue people from intractable disease, the integration of western and oriental medicine is urgently needed. For the purpose of integration, co-operative researches have been carried out between China and Japan since 1978, and the following four research fields have been given priority:

1. Cancer
2. Circulatory diseases
3. Public health
4. Oriental medicine and Kampow science.

In this programme, Chinese medical practices are now enriching western medicine by co-operation with Japanese medical scientists, and, on the other hand, Japanese medicine is attempting to cause improvements through Kampow by co-operation with Chinese Kampow doctors.

It must also be mentioned that western countries now pay growing attention to traditional oriental medicine. For example, some doctors in the Medical School of the University of Hamburg, West Germany, have been extending their own research on oriental medicine.

56
A Health Education Check-list

A check-list which might be used for building up health education resources. This is partly based on a Central Health Education Unit brochure from Hong Kong.

It is a list of topics and it is suggested that a centre might build up a series of resources on each. There is a considerable advantage in having material available in a number of different media if funds permit. In this way users can choose the media they want when borrowing from the centre. The types of media are: audio-tape, video-tape, pamphlets, posters (large and small), booklets, slides (with script), films (8 mm and 16 mm).

Theme	*Topic titles and possible content*
1. Dimensions of the body	a. Physical, mental, intellectual, spiritual health
2. The human body	a. How its parts work together
3. Miracle of life	a. Fertilization and development of foetus b. The baby
4. The circulatory system	a. The heart – how it works – how to keep it healthy b. Effects of excessive eating, smoking, lack of exercise on heart and life c. Hypertension: causes and management d. Heart disease: prevention, after-care e. The heart attack: care, open heart surgery f. Blood: its composition
5. Respiratory system	a. How we breathe b. Emphysema: relation between smoking and lung function

6. Musculo-skeletal system
   a. How it works
   b. Rheumatoid arthritis: how it affects the body, treatment by rest, heat, exercise, therapy
   c. Neck and back pain: how to avoid through correct posture in standing, sitting, walking, sleeping

7. Endocrine system
   a. Diabetes: causes and treatment

8. Reproductive system and sex education
   a. The coming of puberty (girls' version, boys' version and common version)
   b. Vasectomy
   c. Voluntary tubal sterilization
   d. Venereal disease
   e. Healthy relationships: girl–boy, man–woman

9. Sensory organs
   a. Eyes: how they work, correcting defects, treating injuries
   b. Ears: how they work, correcting defects, treating injuries

10. Dental health
   a. Structure of teeth, plaque formation
   b. Preventive measures: brushing, proper diet, fluoridation, regular check-ups

11. Women's health
   a. Importance of periodic gynaecological examination, self-examination of breasts
   b. Pregnancy and smoking, why there is no good reason for beginning or continuing smoking as a habit
   c. Pre-natal care and exercise
   d. Childbirth, experiences of giving birth, husband's experiences

12. Children's health
   a. Breast feeding, correct feeding of growing baby
   b. Child behaviour, love and discipline
   c. Safety at home
   d. Safety on the road and at school
   e. Keeping clean and neat
   f. Family life

13. Health of the elderly

a. Physical and mental well-being of old people
b. Exercise and posture of the elderly, care of eyes, ears, oral hygiene

c. Continuing social life, useful social role of elderly and "retired"

14. Mental health

a. Coping with stress: what it is, how to recognize it, how to deal with it
b. Positive attitude to life, the role of work, leisure, social and family life

15. Alcohol and drugs

a. The harmful effects of alcohol and drugs
b. Specific films on the dangers and rehabilitation of users of alcohol, marijuana, cocaine, heroine, LSD
c. Rehabilitation of drug addicts, how you and society can help

16. Prevention of accidents

a. Medicines, drugs, poisons
b. Bleeding and what to do
c. Burn emergency
d. Accident prevention at home, on the road, in the place of work

17. Prevention of infectious disease

a. Specific films, tapes, videos, posters, etc, on the infectious diseases prevalent in the area (for example, tetanus, polio, scabies, cholera, leprosy)
b. Germs and what they do
c. The body fighting disease
d. Disease communicated through environmental vectors (for example, malaria through mosquitoes), prevention

18. Food hygiene

a. Rules and regulations in preparing and handling food
b. Food contamination, what it is, how to prevent it
c. Kitchen and dining room hygiene, correct disposal of waste, keeping the environment clean and aesthetically pleasant

290

19. A healthy lifestyle	a. Keeping neat and clean b. Appropriate clothing, footwear, housing, furniture, relationship with climate in the area c. Physical fitness d. Total fitness through a combination of exercises, aerobatic exercises, yoga, meditation, weight-lifting, gymnastics, dance
20. The dimensions of health	a. Individual, family and community health b. Health of body and mind, health and the environment, health and belief, health and ethics c. Traditional modern methods of health care d. Alternative lifestyles, how other cultures live complete and healthy lives, the lessons to be learnt from them.

57

Some Suggestions for a Guide-book to Health

Listed below are some miscellaneous thoughts which might be included in a guide-book for health education. They are meant as a stimulus to help those putting together guide-books to health: it is realized that not everyone will agree with all the statements which have come from different sources.

1. Some Practical Codes for Healthy Living

a. Take responsibility for your own health
b. Ask questions of doctors and teachers
c. Practise what you preach and set an example
d. Look after people around you as well as yourself
e. Never eat or drink an excess of anything
f. Greed leads to disease
g. Report illness as soon as you feel ill – early treatment saves lives.

2. Nutrition

a. Always eat as much raw and fresh vegetables, fruit, salads, seeds, nuts and grains as possible
b. Do not overcook food
c. Avoid tinned or bottled foods containing preservatives, artificial sweeteners and colourings
d. Avoid all rancid foods
e. Balance your intake of food – do not eat a lot of one thing and nothing of another
f. A healthy balance of grain, pulses, nuts, seeds, vegetables, fruit and a small portion of meat is ideal
g. Do not eat large meals late at night

h. Eat several small meals during the day in preference to one large one
i. Do not eat between meals – give your digestive system a rest
j. Do not eat if you are too hot
k. Eat slowly and relax while eating
l. Rest a while after eating
m. Preferably drink before or after, but not during a meal
n. Avoid an excess of protein in your diet
o. Drink pure natural water
p. Eat only when hungry

3. How to Protect Yourself Against Common Poisons in Food, Water, the Air and the Environment

a. If possible, avoid living where the atmosphere is polluted by industrial waste or by fumes from transport.
b. Avoid eating food grown with the aid of excessive amounts of chemicals, insecticides, herbicides, etc.
c. Wash all vegetables and fruit very carefully with warm water before eating them.
d. If using any toxic chemicals in the home, read the instructions carefully.
e. Drink only boiled or pure natural water if there is the smallest danger of water being polluted.
f. A diet should include appropriate amounts of carbohydrate, protein, fats, vitamins and mineral salts. A guide-book to health should include details of what is appropriate for the particular country or region as an appropriate balanced diet can be a good protection against poisons in the environment.

4. Immunization

Vaccination of children can be a most important protection against diseases and any health guide should include details of precisely what is appropriate in a particular country or region.

5. First Aid

All schools and all homes should be encouraged to have a first aid kit and to be instructed in the use of it.

6. Avoid Health-destroying Agents

Any guide should give specific advice on the dangers associated with tobacco and alcohol, and the excessive consumption of coffee, tea, chocolate, cola drinks and even soft drinks. Reference might also be made to excessive use of salt, harmful spices, mustard, black and white pepper, white vinegar and refined white sugar. It would obviously be wise to emphasize the dangers associated with hashish, marijuana, opium, cocaine, heroin and all dangerous drugs.

Index

295